2001

To Elden
From Mom & Dad.

THE MOUNT&
THE MASTER

THE MOUNT & THE MASTER

ROBERT E. WELLS

Deseret Book Company
Salt Lake City, Utah

This book is not an official publication of The Church of Jesus Christ of Latter-day Saints. It has been prepared by the author, and he alone is responsible for the content.

Library of Congress Cataloging-in-Publication Data

Wells, Robert E.
   The Mount and the Master / by Robert E. Wells.
    p. cm
   Includes index.
   ISBN 0-87579-391-6
   1. Sermon on the Mount—Criticism, interpretation, etc.
2. Sermon on the Mount—devotional literature.   3. Book of Mormon.
Nephi, 3rd—Criticism, interpretation, etc.   4. Spiritual life—
Mormon authors.   I. Title.
BT382.W45   1991
226.9'06—dc20   90-19897
                                         CIP

Printed in the United States of America
10   9   8   7   6   5   4   3   2   1

Contents

	Preface	vii
	Acknowledgments	xv
1	Blessed Are the Poor in Spirit	1
2	Blessed Are They That Mourn	15
3	Blessed Are the Meek	28
4	Blessed Are They Who Hunger and Thirst	42
5	Blessed Are the Merciful	52
6	Blessed Are the Pure in Heart	66
7	Blessed Are the Peacemakers	80
8	Blessed Are the Persecuted	90
9	The Salt of the Earth; the Light of the World	100
10	The Five Higher Laws of the Gospel	113
11	The Highest Law of All: Be Ye Perfect	130
12	Three Rules Against Hypocrisy	135
13	Treasures, Serving Two Masters, Seeking the Kingdom of God	149
14	Judge Not That Ye Be Not Judged	162

Contents

15 Ask, Seek, Knock   170

16 The Golden Rule   180

17 The Straight and Narrow Way   185

18 Beware of False Prophets   191

19 He That Doeth the Will of My Father   199

20 Build upon the Rock   207

Bibliography   215

Index   217

Preface

One of the greatest sermons ever given by the Master Teacher, Jesus Christ, is the Sermon on the Mount. This sermon is considered by students of Christianity to be the first relatively full declaration by the Master of the essence of Christian faith and the Christian way of life. It is a blueprint for us to use in our personal path toward perfection, as well as a pattern of many of the attributes and qualities we must develop in our eternal quest to approach the perfection Jesus exemplifies. Therefore, those who would "come unto him" will seek to follow these admonitions and try to make daily progress toward the goal he has so clearly put forth.

The message of this sermon was so important that Jesus declared the same concepts to his followers on the American continent. Fortunately, the second account of this greatest of all sermons is recorded in the Book of Mormon, and we might also conclude that he gave it to other peoples he visited elsewhere. We who have the Book of Mormon account have the opportunity to compare that version with the one recorded in the Bible and to enjoy fully each additional degree of insight or information that comes to light through that comparison.

In order to appreciate the setting when this message was given, it might be well to review some of the things we know about what was happening those many centuries ago near the Sea of Galilee. Elder James E. Talmage, in *Jesus the Christ,*

notes that Matthew mentions the sermon early in his account
of the Savior's life and ministry, placing it even before he tells
about his own call as an apostle. Luke places it after his
ordination. Matthew tells us that Jesus went up a mountain
and that he sat as he taught (it is interesting to note that
other biblical writers tell us that the Jewish custom in the
synagogue was to sit in order to give emphasis to the content
of one's words). Luke records that Jesus and the Twelve descended from the mountain to a plain, and Jesus stood. I enjoy
Elder Talmage's remark: "Critics who rejoice in trifles, often
to the neglect of weightier matters, have tried to make much
of these seeming variations." (See *Jesus the Christ*, 1983 ed.,
note 1, p. 230.) Jesus probably spoke first to the apostles on
the mount and then gave the same sermon to the multitude
at a later time.

The physical setting is not important, but we remember
that Jesus was baptized by John in the Jordan River to fulfill
all righteousness and in order to begin his ministry. He then
probably returned to his home in Nazareth and from there
went to the Sea of Galilee and the city of Capernaum to begin
his ministry—perhaps because he knew it would not be easy
to preach at home, where he was known as the son of Joseph
and Mary. He taught in the synagogues and he healed many
people. The multitudes following him grew. The Matthew
account then says that "seeing the multitudes, he went up
into a mountain," and when he had sat down, he taught them.
(Matthew 5:1–2.)

In my mind, I see a scene of peaceful beauty. It is late
afternoon, softening toward dusk. High, wispy cirrus clouds
stand almost motionless in the clear blue sky. Below, on the
coast of the sea, soft waves slap against moored fishing boats.
The great crowd, sitting on the ground, is hushed. Looking
up at the Lord, they listen to him tell them about the personal
attributes they need to acquire in order to follow him and

achieve eternal life. It is a scene no photographer can accurately capture on film because of its spiritual dimension.

The setting of the sermon in the Americas is very different from that in Galilee. Here some twenty-five hundred believers are gathered at the temple in the land Bountiful. They are the more faithful ones whose lives were spared during the terrible earthquakes and fires and floods at the time of the Crucifixion. They are marveling about these events and talking about the Savior. When they hear a soft voice out of heaven, they do not understand it. They hear the voice again, and still they do not understand. When it speaks a third time, they look toward heaven, and this time they hear Heavenly Father saying, "Behold my Beloved Son, in whom I am well pleased, in whom I have glorified my name—hear ye him." Then they see "a Man descending out of heaven . . . clothed in a white robe." Then, we are told, the Savior comes down and stands "in the midst of them." (3 Nephi 11:7–8.)

This account, which is found in 3 Nephi, chapters 11, 12, and 13, is both moving and beautiful. In it, Jesus gives authority to baptize in his name all who repent of their sins. He counsels the people to stop any disputations and anger. Several times he commands them to have faith in him, to repent, and to be baptized. He calls and commissions twelve apostles. Then he delivers a discourse similar to the Sermon on the Mount.

I will not try to identify any Book of Mormon site with a specific geographical area, so we cannot accurately describe the setting in the Americas with the same detail we can give the New Testament account. However, having traveled the countries where most Latter-day Saint scholars believe the Book of Mormon history unfolded, I do have several favorite sites. In one such location, I saw the ruins of an ancient city with impressive temples, set well above the fertile plain of lush green tropical vegetation. "Islands" of rain forest are intermixed with banana plantations, coconut palms, and green patches of pastures where animals graze peacefully. Abundant water from many streams flows placidly toward the ocean a short distance away. The site of the ruins overlooks a rolling plain that surely could have been called Bountiful, as evidenced by the plentiful harvest of delicious fruits and vegetables still growing there today. Foliage covers most of the ruins: gigantic trees, long, hanging vines, elephant-eared plants, and a profusion of orchids and other flowers. Behind the tallest temple, which is now partially restored, mountains covered with an impenetrable jungle camouflage other lost secrets. In the Americas are many sites similar to this, but I leave them to the imagination, since our faith should be based on the content of the Sermon on the Mount and not on the physical setting. But I can see my Savior descending out of that blue tropical heaven just as clearly as I can see him sitting on a rock on a mount overlooking the Sea of Galilee.

The reader also deserves an explanation as to why each chapter begins with four different versions of the same basic scriptural passage. This is perhaps just a personal preference, but many years ago I found that different translations of the same scripture provided texture and depth to the message. This study led me to greater introspection on the subject and challenged me to arrive at my own conclusion as to which seemed to fit best into my feeling of what the prophets or the Savior originally said.

I have spent over forty years living and working and preaching the gospel in Latin America, speaking in Spanish and some Portuguese. I have studied languages enough to know that many words or ideas are not presently translatable and must await the perfection of the Adamic language. Therefore, I do not expect a perfect translation of any one language into another except when a prophet is translating as a seer and revelator and divine translator. First, the Book of Mormon version is cited because the records that the Prophet Joseph Smith translated are, to my mind, the only pure and absolutely correct translations. The King James Version is shown also, because that is the Bible we as Latter-day Saints accept and use, even though we believe that some of the material may be missing or may not have been translated correctly. I use the Jerusalem Bible translation because I have found it to be the translation most similar to the Spanish scriptures we use in the Church (A.D. 1602 Cipriano de Valera version). And finally, I have selected the Phillips Modern Bible translation as a version that often gives different words to compare with the King James Version, while maintaining the integrity of the subject.

The chapters of this book are organized in the order in which the principles are taught in the Matthew account of the Sermon on the Mount. Not all verses are included, but rather a selection has been made with the purpose of identifying those thoughts which are intended for our own personal challenge to follow Christ. Points of doctrine are therefore not included, although they are important. After quoting at the beginning of each chapter the various versions of the scripture to be discussed, I present an introduction to the subject and then add ideas, experiences, and other information to support the principle given.

The narrative begins, as does the Sermon itself, with the Beatitudes. These eight blessings were not passive philosophical suggestions; rather, they were perceived as somewhat revolutionary: "Blessed are the poor . . . blessed are the meek . . . blessed are the persecuted." If these are blessings, what might condemnations be from this new teacher? But God's ways are not man's ways, and his wisdom is not our wisdom. There is a good explanation in support of why each one of these is a blessing. The Beatitudes are requirements for salvation, and as such, they are commandments to every person who wants to follow in the footsteps of the Savior, our Redeemer. They are also promises to which blessings are attached, contingent upon one's obedience. Stated in another way, "There is a law, irrevocably decreed in heaven before the foundations of this world, upon which all blessings are predicated — and when we obtain any blessing from God, it is by obedience to that law upon which it is predicated." (D&C 130:20–21.) The Lord states that he is bound, or under contract to bless us, when we obey his commandments. (D&C 82:10.)

In the Book of Mormon recording of the first beatitude, we find an addition that carries a universal application. This addition is so important that I have chosen to add it to each of the eight beatitudes and to every one of the other twelve points in this book — the phrase "who come unto me." The Savior said, "Blessed are the poor in spirit *who come unto me.*" (3 Nephi 12:3; italics added.) This important phrase changes the meaning from a relatively passive blessing to a requirement of action upon which the blessing is predicated. It is not enough just to be "poor in spirit." Rather, we must turn to Christ and his saving grace after all we can do. If those who are poor in spirit are to be blessed if they come unto Christ, it would seem that likewise those who mourn, who are persecuted, who are meek, and so on, will be blessed if they, too, come unto Christ.

The stated purpose of the Book of Mormon is to convince people that Jesus is the Christ, a theme that is repeated by virtually all of the writers of that sacred book. As representative of the many passages to that effect, I will quote from Moroni's farewell to the Lamanites: "I would exhort you that ye would come unto Christ. . . . Yea, come unto Christ, and be perfected in him." (Moroni 10:30, 32.)

The mission of The Church of Jesus Christ of Latter-day Saints is to bring to Christ, through the process of faith, repentance, and baptism, those who are not members of the Church, and to bring to Christ, through their becoming more like him, those who are members. We can help redeem our ancestors as well by performing for them here in mortality the saving ordinances, thus opening the door for them to accept Christ in the spirit world. All of this involves coming unto Christ.

Another theme of the Sermon on the Mount is that we are to perfect ourselves by becoming submissive to God's will. If we follow Christ's example and live in accordance with his teachings, happiness and peace will come, even though sometimes we must go against the common current of popular thinking. In other words, we should not do as the world would have us do, if it is at variance with what Christ did and what he wants us to do. Part of the inspiration of the sermon is that it teaches us to lay aside those things which do not contribute to our progress toward eternal life and exaltation. Instead, we are encouraged to sacrifice, to deny ourselves, and to render service to others. We must do his will rather than our own. Self-control will lead to Christ, but that means giving up the things of the world and changing our thoughts, our words, our actions, our habits, our very heart and character in order to become like him and to think like him. Then we will eventually be worthy to be with him eternally.

Acknowledgments

I wish to recognize and thank my wife, Helen, for editing my rough manuscript, for polishing it, and for adding sufficient of her own wisdom that she should have co-author status. It has been a joint project that never would have been possible without her encouragement and technical help and skill.

In addition, I want to thank two dear missionary companions, Mark Zobrist and Dennis Peters, who donated a Laptop word processor that made it possible to write easily while I was in airports, on airplanes, and at home. This contribution has made it possible for me to write in spare moments and then be able to pass the chapter to a floppy disk, which Helen would then edit and print out. Also, my daughter Elayne, a former staff writer for the *Church News,* deserves recognition for her professional review of the manuscript.

No credit list would be complete without thanking Eleanor Knowles for her personal encouragement regarding the concept of the book, the style, and the chapter layout, and invaluable suggestions that immeasureably improved the final product.

Blessed Are the Poor in Spirit

Book of Mormon: *"Yea, blessed are the poor in spirit who come unto me, for theirs is the kingdom of heaven."* (3 Nephi 12:3.)

King James Version: *"Blessed are the poor in spirit: for theirs is the kingdom of heaven."* (Matthew 5:3.)

Jerusalem Bible: *"How happy are the poor in spirit; theirs is the kingdom of heaven."*

Phillips Modern English Bible: *"How happy are those who know their need for God, for the kingdom of Heaven is theirs!"*

Much has been written about the blessings of being poor. The Savior was a carpenter, as was his earthly father, Joseph, so Jesus' family were likely not affluent. He understood what it meant to live simply and frugally. When he was upon the cross, the soldiers gambled for the only material article he had that was of any value — a seamless robe. Many of today's poor identify with Christ and know that he understands their plight.

The Savior also does not deal favorably with the rich who have their focus on worldly possessions. He finds many of them lacking in humility and spirituality. He said, "A rich man shall hardly enter into the kingdom of heaven." (Matthew 19:23.) To impress the lesson more thoroughly, he applied one of the figurative proverbs of that day, saying, "It is easier for a camel to go through the eye of a needle, than for a rich man to enter into the kingdom of God." (Matthew 19:24.)

1

What prompted this statement from the Savior was that a rich young man asked him how he might inherit eternal life. The man's question may give us a clue as to how he obtained his riches: he did not ask how to work for this blessing but rather how to inherit it. After a short conversation, the Savior listed some specific commandments that the young man should live. In simplicity and without apparent pride, the youth said that he had kept all of these commandments and then asked what else he should do. The Master, with love but with powerful insight, stated the one thing the rich young man did not expect. He said, "If thou wilt be perfect, go and sell [all] that thou hast, and give to the poor, and thou shalt have treasure in heaven: and come and follow me." (Matthew 19:21.)

Luke tells us the young man was a ruler—perhaps a high official of the local synagogue or possibly even a member of the Sanhedrin. For him to give up position, honors, and status, and to go on a mission, follow the Savior and do his bidding, was more than this man could do because "he had great possessions." (Matthew 19:22.)

Spirituality is closely related to seeking first the kingdom of heaven. (See chapter 13.) Spirituality increases when one does not seek riches. Seeking to come unto Christ must be our first priority; then, if we obtain much of this world's goods, we will surely use them in the way the Lord has outlined.

Other accounts in the scriptures also indicate that the Savior had a dark view of the rich and tended to exalt the poor. His story of Lazarus and the rich man is a pointed example. (See Luke 16:19–31.) I would like to paraphrase a bit of the interpretation of Elder James E. Talmage. (See *Jesus the Christ,* 1983, pp. 433–36.) Elder Talmage presents Lazarus and the rich man as extremes of contrast between wealth and destitution. The rich man was clothed in the costliest attire; his everyday meals were sumptuous feasts. Lazarus, on the other hand, although honored in the scriptures with a name while the rich man was not, was a poor, helpless beggar, sick and covered with sores.

Then the scene changes dramatically. The same two men are on the other side of the veil, both having died. Lazarus's festering body was probably thrown into a pauper's unmarked grave, while the rich man probably was given an elaborate funeral with pomp and ceremony befitting his status. He is now suffering in hell, but angels have borne Lazarus's immortal spirit up to paradise. Their roles and conditions are completely reversed from what they were on earth.

The rich man, tormented by the hot flames of hell and seeing Lazarus in comfort, cradled symbolically in "Abraham's bosom," pleads for relief and asks that Lazarus come to him with a tiny bit of water to cool his tongue. But the great principle of compensation is explained to him by Abraham in these words: "Son, remember that thou in thy lifetime received thy good things, and likewise Lazarus evil things: but now he is comforted, and thou art tormented." (Luke 16:25.) There are a lot of lessons to be learned from this parable. Apparently in the Savior's mind, those who are rich and who are also selfish and proud can look forward to a time of torment after death, while many of those faithful ones who have suffered poverty and afflictions and wretchedness in this life can look forward to compensation in the next, with freedom from sickness, hunger, oppression, and torment.

We should point out that the rich man's fate was not necessarily the consequence of hard work and the success and goals he achieved, nor was the paradise of Lazarus totally the reward of his poverty. Evidently the rich man failed to use his wealth properly and gave in to self-indulgence and sensuous enjoyment of earthly things to the exclusion of concern for the needs of his fellowmen. Conversely, Lazarus apparently obeyed the commandments and worked hard when he had good health, and in every way he deserved the blessings he received.

The Joseph Smith translation of James 2:1–9 adds the following illustration of the Savior's compassion toward those who are poor:

"My brethren, ye cannot have the faith of our Lord Jesus Christ, the Lord of glory, and yet have respect to persons. For if there come unto your assembly a man with a gold ring, in goodly apparel, and there come in also a poor man in vile raiment; and ye have respect to him that weareth the gay clothing, and say unto him, Sit thou here in a good place; and say to the poor, Stand thou there, or sit here under my footstool: are ye not then in yourselves partial judges, and become evil in your thoughts?

"Hearken, my beloved brethren, Hath not God chosen the poor of this world rich in faith, and heirs of the kingdom which he hath promised to them that love him? But ye have despised the poor. Do not rich men oppress you, and draw you before the judgment seats? Do not they blaspheme that worthy name by the which ye are called? If ye fulfil the royal law according to the scripture, Thou shalt love thy neighbour as thyself, ye do well: but if ye have respect to persons, ye commit sin, and are convinced of the law as transgressors."

To be poor in spirit means to be humble, teachable, contrite, meek, obedient. As the Phillips Modern Translation states, the meek are those who "know their need for God." To be poor in spirit is to recognize that we are not self-sufficient spiritually (or materially, for that matter), but rather that we are always in debt to our Heavenly Father, from whom all blessings flow. In fact, our posture before our God is as the needy, even as beggars. President Harold B. Lee spoke on this subject in the following way:

"To be poor in spirit is to feel yourselves as the spiritually needy, even dependent upon the Lord for your clothes, your food, the air you breathe, your health, your life; realizing that no day should pass without fervent prayer of thanksgiving, for guidance and forgiveness and strength sufficient for each day's need. If a youth realizes his spiritual need, when in dangerous places where his very life is at stake, he may be drawn close to the fountain of truth and be prompted by the Spirit of the Lord in his hour of greatest trial. It is indeed a sad thing for one, because of his wealth or learning or worldly position, to think himself independent of this spiritual need. [Poor in spirit] is the opposite of pride or self-conceit. To the worldly rich it is that 'he must possess his wealth as if he possessed it not' and be willing to say without regret, if he were suddenly to meet financial disaster, as did Job, 'The Lord gave, and the Lord hath taken away; blessed be the name of the Lord.' (Job 1:21.) Thus, if in your humility you sense your spiritual need, you are made ready for adoption into the 'church of the First-born,' and to become 'the elect of God.' " (*Stand Ye in Holy Places,* pp. 343–44.)

Elder Bruce R. McConkie made a statement that combines these two thoughts — that of not being encumbered by much of this world's goods (maybe the poor do have a spiritual advantage) and of being poor in spirit. He quoted Luke, "To the poor the gospel is preached" (Luke 7:22), and James, "Hath not God chosen the poor of this world rich in faith, and heirs of the kingdom which he hath promised to them that love him?" (James 2:5).

He continued, "The poor in spirit! If they come unto Christ, salvation is theirs; and it is so often easier for those who are not encumbered with the cares and burdens and riches of the world to cast off worldliness and set their hearts on the riches of eternity than it is for those who have an abundance of this world's goods." (*The Mortal Messiah* 2:121.)

One of the most powerful scriptures on this attitude is found in the Book of Mormon, where King Benjamin declares that a person must become "a saint through the atonement of Christ the Lord, and [become] as a child, submissive, meek, humble, patient, full of love, willing to submit to all things which the Lord seeth fit to inflict upon him, even as a child doth submit to his father." (Mosiah 3:19.)

President Hugh B. Brown illustrated this principle with his often-quoted classic parable: He had a lovely currant bush in his yard that he had carefully trimmed to be attractive and to produce the best fruit. One day, noticing that it had started to branch out again, he reached for the pruning shears, and as he approached the currant bush, he imagined it to say, "Oh, please don't cut me back. I'm just getting started, and I want to be big like the shade trees." He imagined his response to be: "No, my little bush, I am the gardener here. I have planted you to be a source of fruit and an adornment in this part of my garden, and I am going to prune you back to size."

Many years later, as a colonel in the Canadian forces during World War I, President Brown hoped for an illustrious military career. The next promotion to general should have been his, but when the vacancy occurred, his superiors told him, "We are promoting someone else." He retired to his quarters, crushed with disappointment, and knelt in prayer, asking fervently, "Heavenly Father, why couldn't my prayers have been answered? Haven't I lived up to my covenants? Haven't I done everything I was supposed to do? Why? Why?"

And then he seemed to hear a voice, an echo from the past saying, "I am the gardener here. You were not intended for what you sought to be." Humbled, he then prayed for patience to endure the pruning and to grow and develop as the Lord would have him. (See *An Abundant Life: The Memoirs of Hugh B. Brown,* ed. Edwin P. Firmage, pp. 49, 56–57.)

Both the Joseph Smith Translation and the Book of Mormon accounts of this beatitude indicate that a person who is poor in spirit is blessed when he comes unto Christ and learns to do his will.

Humility is the goal that Alma tried to teach to his son Shiblon when he counseled, "Do not pray as the Zoramites do, for ye have seen that they pray to be heard of men, and to be praised for their wisdom. Do not say: O God, I thank thee that we are better than our brethren; but rather say: O Lord, forgive my unworthiness, and remember my brethren in mercy—yea, acknowledge your unworthiness before God at all times." (Alma 38:13–14.)

This same concept is demonstrated dramatically in the Savior's parable of two men who went into the temple to pray. One was a Pharisee, a member of an ancient Jewish sect that emphasized strict interpretation and observance of the Mosaic law, and the other was a publican, a collector of public taxes in the Roman Empire and rumored to be subject to bribes and other misdeeds. The Pharisee stood and prayed thus: "God, I thank thee, that I am not as other men are, extortioners, unjust, adulterers, or even as this publican. I fast twice in the week, I give tithes of all that I possess." The publican, standing far off, "would not lift up so much as his eyes unto heaven, but smote [himself] upon his breast, saying, God be merciful to me, a sinner." (See Luke 18:10–14.) The Savior said the second went home "justified," or forgiven.

Even today we find some who are like the Pharisee, filled with pride, claiming to be fully active in the Church, holding a temple recommend, doing their home teaching regularly, serving in a visible calling, sitting on the front row, and professing to offend no one. And there are many like the publican, recognizing their sins and imperfections and seeking for help to overcome.

This first of the Beatitudes teaches us that Jesus wants us to follow him and become humble as he was humble. He also wants us to be teachable, which is a manifestation of humility.

I once heard a faithful Latter-day Saint mumble about a new leader, "How can you help someone who already knows everything?" — meaning that the new leader was not humble enough to listen to anyone because he thought he knew it all. The humble have ears to hear and open hearts and open minds. They are like vessels that yearn to be filled, and they learn from everyone around them.

Unfortunately, young people usually are less humble and teachable than their elders; we have to learn some things from the harsh lessons of life. I know of a young married man who was very self-sufficient, successful in his career and business interests, recognized in the community, and honored in various ways of the world. He was also active in the Church, serving in a high-profile leadership position. He told me that he had not learned humility and teachableness until a tragedy in the family caused him to realize how fragile life is and how uncertain the future is. He came to realize that the only security in life is to look beyond the veil to the eternities and measure how your life and values and priorities will stand up there. After the tragedy he became much more teachable, did not consider himself better than anyone else, and learned to find joy through service and sacrifice rather than through the honors of men and the power of position and money.

At general conference in April 1989, President Ezra Taft Benson spoke of the roles that disobedience, selfishness, and contention have in pride. He referred to scriptural passages that point out that the proud are easily offended and hold grudges, do not receive counsel or correction easily, and justify and rationalize their frailties and failures.

"Pride is the universal sin, the great vice," he said. "The antidote for pride is humility — meekness, submissiveness. . . . It is the broken heart and contrite spirit. . . . God will have a humble people."

President Benson said that members can choose to humble

themselves by conquering enmity toward others, receiving counsel and chastisement, forgiving others, rendering selfless service, going on missions and preaching the word that can humble others, going to the temple more frequently, and confessing and forsaking sins and being born of God. "We can choose to humble ourselves by loving God, submitting our will to His, and putting Him first in our lives." (*Ensign,* May 1989, pp. 6–7.)

We have all seen men and women, young and old, who have been afflicted with incurable diseases, stricken down by accidents or illnesses that have ruined promising careers, and who have submitted to suffering and to radical changes in lifestyle. Yet many of these individuals have demonstrated patience and acceptance of the changing circumstances and have in turn helped others through their example and words of encouragement.

One such story of inspiration, a story recorded in the November 1988 *New Era,* is about a beautiful young woman, Diane Ellingson, a promising gymnast who had loved to perform ever since she was a child. Her family couldn't afford to pay for lessons, so she went to the gym herself and convinced the coach to let her work at the gym in exchange for lessons.

> She started training when she was fourteen and a half, a late start by competitive standards, but within a year she was competing against the best in the country. . . . In college she led the University of Utah's women's gymnastics team to their first national collegiate title.
>
> After her eligibility for college competition was up, she decided to go on a national professional tour. . . . She says she knew her gymnastics career was mostly over, but she just wanted to hold on to the thrill of the spotlight and the fun of the sport for as long as she could.
>
> During training for the tour Diane was practicing a vault she'd done thousands of times. She ran toward the vault

just like she had done every other time. She jumped on the springboard like all the other times and flew into the air — just like all the other times. This time was different though. This time she rotated just a little too much. This time when she landed, she broke her neck. The accident put her in the hospital for almost half a year and in a wheelchair for the rest of her life.

That was on December 15, 1981. Diane spent that Christmas and the next five months in the hospital, trying to comprehend a life without gymnastics. After so many years of loving the sport, it was difficult for Diane to adjust.

"I hated being in the hospital, and I felt like I was in prison," says Diane. For one month of the five she was in the hospital, she was in traction and couldn't move at all except when the nurses came in and turned her a few inches every two hours. . . . "When I was first injured I thought for sure that in a month I'd be back on the tour and back in shape. I thought, 'If I have enough faith and believe in God and in myself, I'll be okay.' And I just knew it."

Recovery wasn't quite so easy though, and things seemed to get worse. . . .

Finally Diane came to a turning point. "Near the end of my traction one day I was in the depths of despair. I just felt like I couldn't bear it anymore," Diane says. She asked for a blessing. She knew the power to heal her was present, "but I only wanted that to happen if it was Heavenly Father's will. I had this blessing and I felt the greatest sense of peace. It was like I knew that no matter what happened it would be okay. If I didn't walk away from the hospital there would be a reason for it. I knew that I had always tried my best to live the gospel and do what I was supposed to do, so if anybody was worthy to have that blessing, I was. But from that point on I was a different person. I was totally comforted."

Ironically, one of the biggest aids to her recovery was gymnastics. "I don't know if I could've gotten up again if

I hadn't had that training in gymnastics," she says. "I had a lot of chronic injuries when I was a gymnast that I just had to deal with. It was always down, up, down, up in gymnastics and this was just one more down I had to get up from. Gymnastics to a big degree made me so I could be a champion again."

Being a champion is what Diane is all about. [Her sister] Marie says, "Her attitude's always been, 'If you want it, go for it.' She decided when she was young that she would never give up." . . .

Diane made the decision to return to school to finish her degree on the day she finally realized she would never walk again. She was lying on her bed amid scrapbooks filled with souvenirs and photos of her performances. Tears dripped down her face and splashed on the scrapbook pages. "I just realized right then that things weren't going to get any better. As I lay there crying I thought, 'I can either give up or get on with my life,' and that's when I decided to go back to school and get my degree."

Now she teaches a class of third graders who are just the right height to look her in the eye. . . . [She] also gives fireside talks to teenagers who listen, captivated, as she gives her message of hope and perseverance, without bitterness for what has happened. . . . Her main message is one for potential champions: Don't give up, no matter what happens. . . . Diane says, "It makes me feel really good when people tell me they're going to try harder after they've heard my talk. . . . People always think, 'You're so amazing, you're so incredible,' but I'm not. People will say, 'If that happened to me I could never cope with it,' and the thing I have to say is, 'Either you cope or you die.' You have to take whatever life gives you and deal with it, even if you might not want to. You know, if somebody dies in your family, you have to live with it. If you break your neck you have to live with it, but you just learn and that's what's so great about time and the healing process. You don't have to be miraculous." (Kendra Kasl Phair, "A Champion Again," *New Era*, November 1988, pp. 21–25.)

Moroni, adding a few words of explanation into the record of Ether, says: "I give unto men weakness that they may be humble; and my grace is sufficient for all men that humble themselves before me; for if they humble themselves before me, and have faith in me, then will I make weak things become strong unto them." (Ether 12:27.)

We truly feel more humble when we consider the infinite creations of our Heavenly Father, who declared: "Worlds without number have I created; and I also created them for mine own purpose; and by the Son I created them, which is mine Only Begotten." (Moses 1:33.) Enoch expressed a similar idea: "Were it possible that man could number the particles of the earth, yea, millions of earths like this, it would not be a beginning to the number of thy creations; and thy curtains are stretched out still; and yet thou art there." (Moses 7:30.)

Bishop Henry B. Eyring, of the Presiding Bishopric, shares this insight:

"Because God is so great and I am so small, it is easy to admit what I do not know. Therefore, I am teachable.

"My father was an internationally famous research chemist. When he would give talks to audiences of nonscientists, he would often . . . give his idea of an explanation of a scientific question and then he would laugh and say, 'You know, sometimes I think that God watches me and laughs at me as I struggle like a little child. Someday I will be with Him and He will show me how childlike my ideas were.'

"That always got a chuckle from the audience, and it endeared Dad to people because they thought it was a sign of his humility. It was far more than a sign of humility. It was an explanation of why he was a lifelong learner. . . . He really saw himself as a little child. Because of that, it was easy for him to admit that there were better explanations than the ones he had already offered. He was constantly changing, constantly trying to learn." (Commencement address, Ricks College, April 21, 1988.)

Thirty-five years ago I flew a small single-engine Cessna, its cabin the size of that of a Volkswagen "bug" — and the power not much greater — from New York to Buenos Aires, Argentina. The greatest obstacle on the route was the fearsome Andes mountain range between Chile and Argentina, which has the highest peak on both American continents. My co-pilot and I circled and climbed, and climbed and circled, trying to get enough altitude to begin crossing the Andes through a mountain pass. Low clouds kept the mountains from view, and we knew that without a clear pathway we could not make it. Finally the aircraft was at its absolute ceiling, but we were still blocked by the clouds.

The weather report on our radio indicated that the mountains were clear, so the barrier was just a buildup on the near side of the range. We could not make the crossing on instruments since many peaks were higher than our reachable ceiling, so we decided to poke our nose into the clouds for a fixed number of minutes. If we broke into the clear we would continue; if not, we would turn back. The minutes and seconds ticked by, and just before the limit we broke clear and faced the most awe-inspiring sight I had ever seen. It was spectacular — like a view from a throne of the Gods.

We saw sharp-toothed mountains, snow-covered but blue, stretching left into the distance, and to the right off into infinity. At intervals, giant peaks, crowned with a lenticular cloud denoting high winds and turbulence ahead, rose up to 23,000 feet above us, and we could see the pass beneath us. God's creations had never been grander or more majestic, with a sense of mystery that made us aware of our own puny limitations. We had been somewhat arrogant, feeling that we had conquered the length of the hemisphere, but suddenly we recognized that we needed to humble ourselves before our Creator and acknowledge that it was he who had allowed us to view his works and that we should be grateful and worship him. The mountains spread out before us like an infinite wonder and we knew there was no end to his greatness. I have never fully recovered from that humbling experience. My co-pilot was equally subdued. We continued our journey in silence, silently praising the Lord for the privilege of witnessing his true artistry.

In the Book of Mormon rendering of this beatitude on the poor in spirit, the phrase "who come unto me" has been added. And what an addition it is! This is the primary focus of the gospel today. It is the main focus of the Book of Mormon. The mission of The Church of Jesus Christ of Latter-day Saints is to bring people to Christ. Otherwise, the Atonement holds no validity for them. It is altogether fitting that this most important keystone of the gospel of Christ should be the central theme of the first beatitude. What a shame that this key has been lost for centuries to Christianity! What a joy that it has been restored!

It is appropriate also to note that some modern translations of the Bible have changed the word *blessed* to *happy*. Most people are intrinsically happy a good part of the time, but problems—such as poor health, financial reverses, disappointments, frustrations, guilt, and fear—all occur at times in every life. When these times come, turning to the Savior in faith and love will reward us with affirmations of the spiritual joy and hope we can find in the gospel.

CHAPTER 2

Blessed Are They That Mourn

Book of Mormon: *"And again, Blessed are all they that mourn [who come unto me], for they shall be comforted."* (3 Nephi 12:4.)

King James Version: *"Blessed are they that mourn: for they shall be comforted."* (Matthew 5:4.)

Jerusalem Bible: *"Happy those who mourn: they shall be comforted."*

Phillips Modern English Bible: *"How happy are those who know what sorrow means, for they will be given courage and comfort!"*

This second beatitude appears, at first glance, to be the most unusual and contradictory of all. How can it be a blessing to be in mourning? To mourn usually means to show grief or pain at the death of a loved one. This intense feeling cannot be hidden from the world or from God; it cannot be eased or pacified except with comfort and consolation from God through the Holy Ghost.

Elder James E. Talmage comments that "the mourner shall be comforted for he shall see the divine purpose in his grief." (*Jesus the Christ*, 1983, p. 216.) Perhaps this means that as we bear our sorrows by turning to Christ, and as we sorrow for others, we will become more like Christ, because he sorrowed for the pain of others; as we sorrow for the sins of the world we progress somewhat toward the perfection of him who

15

interceded and became the great sin-bearer for us all. As we mourn, we can see his divine purposes fulfilled in many ways.

So why would the Savior say that it is a blessing to mourn? It might be that pain and suffering at the death of loved ones is an essential part of our mortal experience, one that obliges us to face the question of the reality of the spirit world and the hope of the resurrection. Could it be that through suffering we discover what is eternally important?

On the other hand, it might be that it is a blessing for us to become more fully aware that God's ways are not always our ways, and that we must trust him when things don't go as we believe they should. When we can see the Lord's purposes fulfilled in our times of grief and sorrowing, then the Holy Ghost can console us and the Atonement and the Resurrection can become the cornerstones of our faith.

The traditional interpretation of this beatitude is that Christ is speaking of mourning the death of a loved one. We will treat that aspect first, but we will also discuss the possibility of additional facets of this second beatitude, such as mourning because of our sins, or mourning the sins of the world, or mourning iniquity in general, or mourning ignorance or wars or afflictions.

Mourning the Death of a Loved One

Some students of cultures both ancient and modern philosophize that one important way to measure a culture or civilization is to observe the way they honor their dead — the way they bury them, the way they remember them. For example, some cultures or religions honor and bury a deceased leader with elaborate ceremonies. They may wait weeks for the funeral because of the complexity of the established protocol. Others bury their loved ones within no more than twenty-four hours, because embalming is not available. Some families return regularly to the grave sites of loved ones to place flowers there in remembrance of birthdays, anniversaries, Easter, and other special occasions, while others find it unnecessary or uncomfortable or even impossible to visit the grave sites of loved ones.

Funerals in some instances are short, basic, and spare. Others are long and feature much protocol and ceremony. Which is correct? Which is best? Is there any standard to follow?

As with any cultural situation, it is inappropriate to judge one practice against another, saying what is best or what is inferior, appropriate or inappropriate. All we should say is that one is different from another. Feelings are too sensitive to make comparisons or judgments. However, we shall discuss the typical Latter-day Saint funeral.

The purpose of a public or private LDS funeral, whether it is held at a meetinghouse, at a funeral home, or in a private home, is threefold: (1) to honor the dead, (2) to comfort the loved ones, and (3) to worship God, remembering and teaching the Atonement and the Resurrection. In addition to services presided over by the priesthood, there is a private family prayer before the funeral, and a service at the cemetery for loved ones and family members, when the final resting place is dedicated by an authorized person holding the Melchizedek Priesthood, usually a close member of the family.

To honor the dead, we usually have a eulogy that includes the basic facts that history should record about the individual and his or her parents, family, and survivors. We also speak about the person's accomplishments, recognitions, outstanding Christian virtues and values, missions, military service, Church callings, and community service. This is really a time to inspire the living with the best qualities of the person recently deceased.

To comfort the family in their grief, we quote scriptures and the inspiring words of prophets, poets, and philosophers.

We mention discreetly the circumstances or details of the death in such a way as to give insight or understanding, to help ease the grief. Those who have suffered intense pain are now released and are free, so we should accept their passing more easily. Those who have lived a long and full life, dying in their golden years, are relatively easy to speak of and there is less need for comfort because all were ready for the event. It is more difficult to ease grief when death was caused by an accident or the deceased person is young. No one is ever prepared in such situations. These are the times when the doctrines of the gospel of Jesus Christ are most relevant and especially needed. Friends and loved ones need spiritual meat for consolation, not platitudes. The plan of salvation, the true understanding of our relationship with our Heavenly Father, the Savior, and the Holy Ghost, and the assurance that life after death is a reality—all give peace and comfort.

To worship God, who moves in mysterious ways, who gives and who takes away, who knows the beginning from the end; to worship Christ; and to worship the Holy Comforter, who truly comforts—these are important reasons for which we hold funeral services. When we accept God's will, it is easier to be consoled and comforted, but if we are fighting against reality, there is little that the Spirit can do to help. We all must submit to the Father's will, even as a child must submit to his earthly father.

The basic declarations of faith in our Redeemer and in his mission as the Son of God to overcome death and bring about the resurrection of all who have been born are well described by Elder James E. Talmage in his books *Jesus the Christ* and *Articles of Faith*. Especially helpful for funeral sermon preparation are chapter three in *Jesus the Christ*, titled "The Need of a Redeemer," and chapter four in *Articles of Faith*, "The Atonement and Salvation." Those who speak at funerals usually obtain the doctrinal parts of their sermons from such

funerals

18

sources, as well as from the writings and sermons of apostles and members of the First Presidency and from their own study of the scriptures.

To all who have lost a loved one, the promise in this beatitude is the climactic part. They *will* be comforted; the promise is true. Faith and hope lead to consolation and comfort. Those who weep now over the loss of a loved one, after learning or remembering the purposes of the Lord and the role of that brief separation we call death, shall be comforted in time. It is seldom as quick as we would like, but there is wisdom in the Lord in this, and the best healing is that which is thorough and deep. Peace that surpasses understanding is promised to all those who have a testimony and knowledge of the plan of salvation. There is no greater comfort than to know that death is part of the plan of God for this life, and that our departed loved ones shall be part of the family group or circle with us in the life to come. When we can look into the beauty of the family in the next life, we see glories that help heal the wounds of this present estate. When the Savior comes again to rule in glory during the Millennium, he will wipe away our tears and there shall be no more death nor sorrow, crying nor pain. (See Revelation 21:4.)

Fullness of comfort does come from the sure knowledge that the deceased are not dead; they are only separated from us, and their spirits have gone through another door into the hallowed halls of a higher existence, as God intended. They that mourn shall truly be comforted.

When my father died, I was just a little boy. My widowed mother did not easily get over the shock of the unexpected death of her bishop husband. Although I do not remember much of that period, I do remember the deep sorrow and constant grief of my mother. In my mind's eye, I can see so clearly a mental picture of us kneeling in prayer at the bedside or in the woodstove-heated kitchen on the linoleum floor. My mother would pray aloud with my hand in hers. She would pray a bit, then break down and cry. Then she would regain her composure and continue praying. Again she would cry and then pray some more. I grew up knowing what it meant to cry unto the Lord. I still find it easy to shed tears while praying. Later, when I passed through a similar kind of test, I again found that there is no stopping the shedding of tears when a loved one leaves us to pass to the other side of the veil. I also rediscovered that vocal prayer helped more than silent prayer.

The Comforter is near, ready to help, and the burden is bearable. The hope of the Resurrection sustains us, and we can look forward in faith to a glorious reunion in the spirit world and in the Millennium.

The Brazilians have a sad song with lyrics that reflect the deepness and permanence of sorrow, even when one has the gospel and looks forward to the next life. They sing "*Tristeza no tem fin, mas felicidade, si.*" Translated it means "Sadness has no ending; only happiness does." Time does help; time even heals. But, in a way, the mourning is always there. It is hidden, but it erupts now and then in unexpected ways that none of us can control. Yet life goes on and we find new sources of happiness; we know that in the promised resurrection, the lingering mourning caused by temporary separation will disappear.

Since mourning is so universal, the Lord must have a purpose for having us experience it. There is no doubt but that he softens and molds us and touches us most deeply when we are mourning. He led Israel in the wilderness for forty years of suffering and afflictions in order to humble them. In the Old Testament we are told that as a man chasteneth his son, so the Lord our God will chasten us. (See Deuteronomy 8:2–3, 5.) In the chastening, or in an event that causes us so much sorrow and grief, he can reach us and talk to us about his divine purposes and plan.

It appears that Heavenly Father never expected us to walk through life with uninterrupted, Garden of Eden innocence and pleasure. There is no such thing as a life of continual plains of smooth happiness.

God created a life in which we would face tests and trials and tribulations. Christ said, "In the world ye shall have tribulation." But he assured us that "in me ye might have peace." (John 16:33.) He planned this world to include frustrations, anxieties, difficulties, and other tests, such as death of loved ones, terminal illnesses, and fatal accidents. Out of our difficult experiences, we will have the opportunity for genuine growth and development of a Christlike character.

Job tells us that there is divine purpose behind grief and suffering: "Behold, happy is the man whom God correcteth: therefore despise not thou the chastening of the Almighty: for he maketh sore, and bindeth up: he woundeth, and his hands make whole." (Job 5:17–18.) Job knew that suffering sometimes causes bitterness and a kind of poison in the individual. He also seemed to be aware that in one life difficulty can ennoble, while in another life the same difficulty will cause depreciation. It is our responsibility to handle sorrow in a positive way and not let it destroy us. We are being tested. Our reaction to sorrow is perhaps more important than what is happening to our loved one who has gone on before. That individual is all right. We are the ones to be concerned about. We ought to ask, What is God trying to teach me now? What am I to learn about myself? The answer is: Come unto Christ — now more than ever.

To Mourn for One's Own Sins

Another aspect of mourning that we might consider in connection with this beatitude is mourning for our own sins. Perhaps we can learn something from the example of David. He sincerely grieved and pleaded for forgiveness after he had sinned with the wife of Uriah. His tragic lament is quoted here in part: "Have mercy upon me, O God, according to thy lovingkindness: according unto the multitude of thy tender mercies blot out my transgression. Wash me thoroughly from mine iniquity, and cleanse me from my sin. . . . Purge me with hyssop, and I shall be clean: wash me, and I shall be whiter than snow. . . . Hide thy face from my sins, and blot out all mine iniquities. Create in me a clean heart, O God; and renew a right spirit within me. . . . Restore unto me the joy of thy salvation; and uphold me with thy free spirit." (Psalm 51:1–2, 7, 9–10, 12.)

All our sins are to be deeply mourned by us, and surely by those who love us the most and who are thus affected by our acts. David poured out his soul on behalf of all who mourn for their sins. But also David spoke for all in an eloquent way when, in Psalm 32, he spoke of the blessings of being forgiven (if we are truly repentant). It is almost like another beatitude: "Blessed is he whose transgression is forgiven, whose sin is covered. Blessed is the man unto whom the Lord imputeth not iniquity, and in whose spirit there is no guile." (Psalm 32:1–2.)

The great leader David had fallen in sin. He had cried out in remorse and desperation. He seems to have mourned most because he had sinned against God, who had given so much to him. He really wanted to be forgiven, and the words seem to fit the promise, "Blessed is he whose transgression is forgiven."

President Harold B. Lee had some thoughts which further illuminate this concept:

"To mourn, as the Master's lesson here would teach, one must show that 'godly sorrow that worketh repentance' (2 Corinthians 7:10) and wins for the penitent a forgiveness of sins and forbids a return to the deeds of which he mourns. It is to see, as did the Apostle Paul, "glory in tribulations . . . knowing that tribulation worketh patience; and patience, experience; and experience, hope.' (Romans 5:3–4.) You must be willing 'to bear one another's burdens, that they may be light." (Mosiah 18:8.) You must be willing to 'mourn with those that mourn, and comfort those that stand in need of comfort.' (Mosiah 18:9.) When a mother mourns in her loneliness for the return of a wayward daughter, you with compassion must forbid the casting of the first stone. . . . In a word, you must be as the publican and not as the Pharisee. 'God be merciful to me a sinner.' (Luke 18:13.) Your reward for so doing is the blessedness of comfort for your own soul through a forgiveness of your own sins." (*Stand Ye in Holy Places*, p. 344.)

To Mourn for the Sins of Others

In the Old Testament, we find the example of the prophet Daniel, who mourned for the sins of all of Judah. He felt the burden of all and recounted those sins for which he lamented. Following are some of his words taken from the ninth chapter of Daniel: "I set my face unto the Lord God, to seek by prayer and supplications, with fasting, and sackcloth, and ashes. . . . We have sinned, and have committed iniquity, and have done wickedly, and have rebelled, even by departing from thy precepts and from thy judgments: neither have we hearkened unto thy servants the prophets, which spake in thy name. . . . Neither have we obeyed the voice of the Lord our God, to walk in his laws, which he set before us by his servants the prophets. Yea, all Israel have transgressed thy law, even by departing, that they might not obey thy voice. . . . For our sins, and for the iniquities of our fathers, Jerusalem and thy people are become a reproach to all that are about us. . . . O my God, incline thine ear, and hear; open thine eyes, and behold our desolations. . . . O Lord; hear, O Lord, forgive; O Lord, hearken and do."

The prophets all cry unto God with broken hearts for the sins of the people. The Savior himself cried over the sins of the people. He tried to gather them as a hen gathers her chickens, but they would not. Our Heavenly Father grieves most of all, I am sure.

When we, the sinners, mourn for our sins and the sins of those about us, there is the promise of consolation. After Daniel mourned for the sins of the people, the Lord consoled him by telling him, through the angel Gabriel, that the Savior was coming, and he even spoke of the second coming of the Savior. It was of great consolation to him in his mourning to learn of the resurrection of the just to everlasting life. (See Daniel 12.)

In the Book of Mormon we read of Nephi, son of Helaman, who mourned the sins of the once righteous people of Nephi, "seeing the people in a state of such awful wickedness, and those Gadianton robbers filling the judgment-seats—having usurped the power and authority of the land; laying aside the commandments of God, and not in the least aright before him; doing no justice unto the children of men; condemning the righteous because of their righteousness; letting the guilty and the wicked go unpunished because of their money. . . .

"And when Nephi saw it, his heart was swollen with sorrow within his breast; and he did exclaim in the agony of his soul: . . . I am consigned that these are my days, and that my soul shall be filled with sorrow because of this the wickedness of my brethren."

Then Nephi went up on a tower to pour out his soul unto God, and multitudes of people gathered together so they might know the cause of such great mourning. "Why have ye gathered yourselves together? . . . Because I have got upon my tower that I might pour out my soul unto my God, because of the exceeding sorrow of my heart, which is because of your iniquities! And because of my mourning and lamentation ye have gathered yourselves together, and do marvel." (Helaman 7:4–6, 9, 13–15.)

The prophet after whom the Book of Mormon was named mourned the exceedingly great sins of the people of his time. He said: "A continual scene of wickedness and abominations has been before mine eyes ever since I have been sufficient to behold the ways of man. And wo is me because of their wickedness; for my heart has been filled with sorrow because of their wickedness." (Mormon 2:18–19.) We can feel the depth of his sorrow, almost unbearable as he mourns their willful transgressions: "My soul was rent with anguish, . . . and I cried: O ye fair ones, how could ye have departed from the ways of the Lord! O ye fair ones, how could ye have rejected that Jesus, who stood with open arms to receive you!" (Mormon 6:16–17.)

In his parting testimony, Nephi, the son of Lehi, mourned about those whose hearts were hardened against the Holy Spirit and the messages of the prophets, saying, "I pray continually for them by day, and mine eyes water my pillow by night, because of them." (See 2 Nephi 33:2–3.) Perhaps we would all try harder and live better if we knew how the prophets have mourned over our sins and how the Savior himself has tried personally to bring each one of us to him.

Consolation to Those Who Mourn

The Savior's invitation, "Come unto me," is the true source of consolation and comfort. He says, "Come unto me, all ye that labour and are heavy laden, and I will give you rest. Take my yoke upon you, and learn of me; for I am meek and lowly in heart: and ye shall find rest unto your souls. For my yoke is easy, and my burden is light." (Matthew 11:28–29.) The ultimate promise of the Savior is found in the book of Revelation written by John the Beloved. We have this beautiful hope: "God shall wipe away all tears from their eyes; and there shall be no more death, neither sorrow, nor crying, neither shall there be any more pain." (Revelation 21:4.)

Finally, whether it be mourning over death of loved ones, mourning over sins and transgressions, or mourning what might have been, the source of comfort and consolation is always to come unto Christ and to follow him and obey his commandments. Then, we are assured we shall receive peace in our hearts, the Holy Ghost as our companion, and consolation to our soul.

Our Heavenly Father is not an absentee God, nor is Jesus dead. They are relevant today as never before, and if we find them more during times of sorrow than ever before, we are blessed. In modern-day revelation we have been given this assurance:

"Whosoever among you are sick, and have not faith to be healed, but believe, shall be nourished with all tenderness, with herbs and mild food, and that not by the hand of an enemy.

"And the elders of the church, two or more, shall be called, and shall pray for and lay their hands upon them in my name; and if they die they shall die unto me, and if they live they shall live unto me.

"Thou shalt live together in love, insomuch that thou shalt weep for the loss of them that die, and more especially for those that have not hope of a glorious resurrection.

"And it shall come to pass that those that die in me shall not taste of death, for it shall be sweet unto them; and they that die not in me, wo unto them, for their death is bitter.

"And again, it shall come to pass that he that hath faith in me to be healed, and is not appointed unto death, shall be healed. He who hath faith to see shall see. He who hath faith to hear shall hear. The lame who hath faith to leap shall leap.

And they who have not faith to do these things, but believe in me, have power to become my sons; and inasmuch as they break not my laws thou shalt bear their infirmities." (D&C 42:43–52.)

And to those who qualify through their righteousness and compliance with certain required ordinances, these promises are given: "Ye shall come forth in the first resurrection . . . and shall inherit thrones, kingdoms, principalities, and powers, dominions, all heights and depths . . . ; and [ye] shall pass by the angels, and the gods, which are set there, to [your] exaltation and glory in all things. . . . This is eternal lives — to know the only wise and true God, and Jesus Christ, whom he hath sent." (D&C 132:19, 24.)

CHAPTER 3

Blessed Are the Meek

Book of Mormon: *"Blessed are the meek [who come unto Christ], for they shall inherit the earth."* (3 Nephi 12:5.)

King James Version: *"Blessed are the meek: for they shall inherit the earth."* (Matthew 5:5.)

Jerusalem Bible: *"Happy the gentle; they shall have the earth for their heritage."*

Phillips Modern English Bible: *"Happy are those who claim nothing, for the whole earth will belong to them!"*

In our modern, materialistic world, we do not usually think of successful leaders or outstanding, gifted individuals as meek. Nor can we accept in our minds the image of a meek, successful quarterback of our favorite football team. In fact, success in any endeavor, be it business, sports, professions, entertainment, or any other area where a leader surfaces, seems to require attributes that are the opposite of meekness.

The usual description of a meek person is one who is compliant, timid, nonassertive, weak, submissive, cowardly; one who seeks nothing, accomplishes nothing, and contributes nothing to society. The world looks down on the meek and the quality of meekness with lofty disdain. But God's ways are not man's ways. And even if the world does not count meekness high on its list of desirable qualities, this should not deter us from seeking to develop every quality that the Savior recommended and exemplified.

28

Perhaps our modern interpretation of *meek* is not what the Savior had in mind two thousand years ago. The Spanish language has a common usage of the expression *meek* in the word *manso*. It gives us a completely different meaning, which is illustrated in a personal experience.

In the lush pampas of Argentina I once visited a 100,000-acre ranch where the owner raised choice grass-fed beef. His hobby was raising and training thoroughbred horses to be used for racing, polo, and for use on the ranch by the *gauchos* (cowboys). The ranch had over one thousand of these beautiful animals, each with its pedigree, each well trained or in the process. The ranch's reputation was such that there was a demand for its horses all over the world at premium prices.

I asked the owner if we would be able to see a rodeo, similar to the rodeos held in the western part of the United States, in which the *gauchos* would break horses. He was aghast. "Not on this ranch you won't!" was his emphatic response. "Since our horses, and especially the polo ponies, have to be lightning fast, fearless, and courageous on the playing field, instantly obedient to every hint of a command and superbly maneuverable, we would never 'break' a horse — we do not want to break his spirit. We love our horses and we work patiently with them until they are *manso*." *Manso* means meek, but here was a new meaning for the word. He explained, "Our *manso* horses are full of fire and spirit, but they are obedient and well trained."

So meek can mean obedient and well trained, an added spiritual application to the words of the Savior. The Savior did not mean for us to be doormats — he certainly was not one. Rather, I think he meant that we should be obedient and well-trained. We can be strong, enthusiastic, talented, spirited, zealous, and bold, and still be meek — obedient and well trained — and able to coexist in the success-oriented world in which we live.

The Argentine horse trainer who used the word *manso* for meek also uses that word to mean tame. The Spanish dictionary shows both interpretations. Tame could also be what the Savior had in mind when speaking of meekness. An illustration of this is found in a classic story, *The Little Prince*. The little prince visits several different planets, and on his visit to the earth he meets a fox.

"Come and play with me," proposes the little prince. "I am so unhappy."

"I cannot play with you," the fox says. "I am not tamed."

"What does that mean . . . tamed?"

"It is an act too often neglected," explains the fox. "It means to establish ties."

"To establish ties?"

"Just that," says the fox. "To me you are still nothing more than a boy who is just like a hundred thousand other little boys. And I have no need of you. And you, on your part, have no need of me. To you, I am nothing more than a fox like a hundred thousand other foxes. But, if you tame me, then we shall need each other. To me, you will be unique in all the world. To you, I shall be unique in all the world." (Antoine de Saint-Exupéry, *The Little Prince*, pp. 65–66.)

Perhaps the Savior had in mind that he could tame us or that we should tame each other. To tame an animal usually involves giving lots of patience, love, affection, rewards, and reinforcement. Don't we need those same qualities in our development of a more Christlike character? Don't we all need to show a lot more patience, love, and affection, to offer more rewards, to feel more concern, and to be more caring toward all the human beings around us? Would not both we and they then be more tame? Is not Christ our example?

In the large cities I have lived in, such as New York, Buenos Aires, Sao Paulo, and Mexico City, people often live next to each other but do not really know each other. There is an aloofness bordering on wildness—because they do not need each other—and they are often not tamed in their inter-relationships. But if we would treat each other as the Savior would have us treat each other—as sons and daughters of God and therefore as brothers and sisters—we would come to need each other, and each friendship would be unique. The greatest tragedy is that there are families in which blood brothers and sisters treat each other without consideration and as if neither had been tamed. *Manso*, tamed, and meek are all good expressions to reflect the tender feelings, qualities, and interrelationships the Savior wants us to have toward each other.

After reading about meekness in the Beatitudes, a humorist once quipped, "The meek are so meek that the only way they might get some of this earth *is* to inherit it—they won't get it any other way." Elder Bruce R. McConkie met this frivolous attitude with a more spiritual thought. He wrote, "As things are now constituted, the meek do not inherit the earth; even He who said of himself, 'I am meek and lowly of heart' (Matt. 11:29) had in fact no place of his own to lay his head. This world's goods were of little moment to him, and he had neither gold nor silver nor houses nor lands nor kingdoms. Peter was even directed to catch a fish in whose mouth a coin was lodged, that a levied tax might be paid for the two of them. The meek—those who are the God-fearing and the righteous—seldom hold title to much of that which appertains to this present world. But there will be a day when the Lord shall come to make up his jewels; there will be a day when Abraham, Isaac, and Jacob, and the faithful of ancient Israel shall dwell again in old Canaan; and there will be also an eventual celestial day when 'the poor and the meek of the earth shall inherit it.' (D&C 88:17.)" (*The Mortal Messiah* 2:122.)

Sooner or later we shall see all of the words of the prophets fulfilled. The time will come, as Elder McConkie declared, when eternal values will prevail and that which the world demeans today will yet be recognized for an eternal value or attribute that we must develop in ourselves if we are to truly come unto Christ. Those who are meek submit themselves to the will of God and therein find new strength and new power.

Submissiveness to God is not a weakness; it represents the learning of an eternal principle. In his great temple sermon, King Benjamin says that the person who is submissive to God "yields to the enticings of the Holy Spirit, and putteth off the natural man and becometh a saint through the atonement of Christ the Lord, and becometh as a child, submissive, meek, humble, patient, full of love, willing to submit to all things which the Lord seeth fit to inflict upon him, even as a child doth submit to his father." (Mosiah 3:19.)

In his sermon on the priesthood, Alma gives a summary of things we should do in order to "be lifted up [unto Christ] at the last day and enter into his rest." We should—

1. Cast off our sins.

2. Not procrastinate our repentance.

3. Humble ourselves before God, and call on his holy name.

4. Watch and pray continually, so that we are not tempted above that which we can bear.

5. Follow the Holy Spirit, becoming humble, meek, submissive, patient, full of love and all long-suffering.

6. Have faith in the Lord.

7. Have a hope that we shall receive eternal life.

8. Have the love of God always in our hearts. (See Alma 13:27-29.)

The quality of meekness is usually associated with a number of other desirable qualities, such as those listed above, and all are related to humility. Alma, in speaking to his son Helaman, gives a short list that includes both meekness and humility: "Preach . . . repentance, and faith on the Lord Jesus Christ;

teach [the people] to humble themselves and to be meek and lowly in heart." (Alma 37:33.)

President Spencer W. Kimball related humility and meekness in a talk at Brigham Young University on January 16, 1963: "[The Savior] gave in his Beatitudes, 'Blessed are the meek: for they shall inherit the earth.' . . . He was saying that only those who are humble enough to forgo the vain glories of the world and to follow the paths of righteousness — paths which may be hard and unpopular — will possess the earth. When the earth is renewed and receives its paradisiacal glory only those will possess the real estate of this celestialized orb who have been meek enough to follow the lowly Nazarene and bravely meet all the problems of life and surmount them. 'Blessed are the meek.' If the Lord was meek and lowly and humble, then to become humble one must do what he did in boldly denouncing evil, bravely advancing righteous work, courageously meeting every problem, becoming the master of himself and the situations about him and being . . . oblivious to personal credit.

"Humility is not pretentious, presumptuous, or proud. It is not weak, vacillating, or servile. . . . Humble and meek properly suggest virtues, not weaknesses. They suggest a consistent mildness of temper and an absence of wrath and passion. Humility suggests no affectation, no bombastic actions. It is not turbid or grandiloquent. It is not servile submissiveness. It is not cowed or frightened. No shadow or the shaking of a leaf terrorizes it.

"How does one get humble? To me, one must constantly be reminded of his dependence. On whom dependent? On the Lord. How remind one's self? By real, constant, worshipful, grateful prayer.

" 'How can I remain humble?' the brilliant missionary asks. By reminding one's self frequently of his own weaknesses and limitations, not to the point of depreciation, but an evaluation guided by an honest desire to give credit where credit is due.

"Humility is teachableness . . . an ability to realize that all virtues and abilities are not concentrated in one's self. . . . Humility is never accusing nor contentious. It is not boastful, because when one becomes conscious of his great humility, he has already lost it. When one begins boasting of his humility, it has already become pride, the antithesis of humility." (*Improvement Era*, August 1963, pp. 656–57, 704.)

President Kimball closed that great address with a statement that came from his own deep wisdom and meditation on this subject:

> Humility is royalty without a crown,
> Greatness in plain clothes,
> Erudition without decoration,
> Wealth without display,
> Power without scepter or force,
> Position demanding no preferential rights,
> Greatness sitting in the congregation,
> Prayer in closets and not in corners of the street,
> Fasting in secret without publication,
> Stalwartness without a label,
> Supplication upon its knees,
> Divinity riding an ass.

President Kimball was that kind of a prophet, and in his humility and meekness there was true greatness.

One of the outstanding qualities of a meek person is the desire to learn the will of God concerning oneself and then to obey that will, be it from a vision, a revelation, the words of a prophet, the still small voice, or an authorized leader — whatever manner God chooses to reveal his will. Christ, as always, is the supreme example. In Gethsemane he prayed: "O my Father, if it be possible, let this cup pass from me:

nevertheless not as I will, but as thou wilt." (Matthew 26:39.) When we ask or knock and the Lord opens the door, we must be willing to walk through it. When we pray for inspiration, we should listen and heed and follow the answer.

To submit to the will of God requires a great deal of trust and faith. Those who are meek trust God and his plan of salvation and the meaning and purpose of this world in which we find ourselves. They trust the account of the premortal existence, the Creation, and the Fall; the need for a Savior and this life of testing and a day of judgment. They trust the need for a Redeemer and understand the Redeemer's place in God's plan.

The development of a healthy personality in today's complex world requires a sense of trust in the God-created universe, a universe with meaning and destiny and eternal absolutes. When we trust in God and obey his will, we can be free from many of the fears that weaken us. In this sense, meekness is a source of strength and power because it leads us to God and teaches us his will for us. When we know truly that God has a plan for us, everything seems to fit into place.

In the life of each Church leader, there are instances in which that individual desires to know the will of the Lord and, after seeking faithfully, is given the answer. But trust and faith are needed if the person is to *do* the Lord's will. That is the sign of meekness. Sometimes it is a strong impression, such as, "Go on your mission *now.*" Those who heed the prompting and go are much blessed. At times, it is a soft inner voice saying, "Study this career instead of the one you planned on." Door after door is opened to those who are faithful, trusting, and obedient.

My own career came about as a fortuitous combination of circumstances, none of which would have been possible had I not followed the whisperings of the Spirit as to my mission and my studies. Likewise, the choosing of an eternal companion is one of the greatest decisions any of us can ever make; and I feel that had I not placed total trust in the whisperings of the Spirit, I would not have been led to my companion, Helen.

I believe that the Lord will prove us thoroughly until he is determined that we will serve him faithfully, no matter what the hazard or the sacrifice. He declared, "We will prove them herewith, to see if they will do all things whatsoever the Lord their God shall command them." (Abraham 3:25.) The person who has learned meekness learns how to submit to the will of God even if doing so means inconvenience, sacrifice, change, and much patience, all of which require a supreme act of faith and trust in the will of God.

President Harold B. Lee taught that "a meek [person] is defined as one who is not easily provoked or irritated and is forbearing under injury or annoyance. The meek [person] is the strong, the mighty, the [person] of complete self-mastery. He is the one who has the courage of his moral convictions, despite the pressure of the gang or the club. In controversy his judgment is the court of last resort and his sobered counsel quells the rashness of the mob. He is humble-minded; he does not bluster. 'He that is slow to anger is better than the mighty. . . .' (Proverbs 16:32.) He is a natural leader and is the chosen of army and navy, business and church, to lead where other men follow. He is the 'salt' of the earth and shall inherit it." (*Stand Ye in Holy Places,* p. 346.)

Those who are meek are mild-tempered, not easily provoked to anger or irritation. They are patient and forbearing under injuries, not proud or resentful or full of self-importance. They make effective leaders because they have genuine inner strength. They can reach out with love in dealing with people who are more aggressive.

Those who are meek submit to the will of God and thereby gain power and strength to face and solve the dilemmas of life. They accept the inevitable with exemplary resolve and can adjust to decrees of destiny that they cannot change.

Those who are meek will turn to God in order to learn his will, and they will follow the promptings of the Spirit. Christ, in the Garden of Gethsemane, is our prime example of this. Great strength came to him as he faced his supreme test in which he willingly submitted to the will of the Father. Wise parents try to instill in their children the kind of faith that will enable them to face life's uncertainties. Some child psychologists believe in order to have a healthy personality, children need to develop trust in God and in the order of the universe. This kind of trust will give them strength to banish fear.

Moses was meek. When Jethro intervened with advice on how to organize the kingdom better (see Exodus 18:21–24), Moses was meek enough to listen and put the plan into practice. Those who lack meekness find it difficult to accept advice and to follow suggestions of peers and subordinates, even when those suggestions are brilliant and inspired. In this sense, they also lack the strength that can come from friends, associates, relatives, and others.

Mahatma Gandhi, the great Indian leader, was an unusually meek but strong man. Through nonviolence and resistance without direct confrontation, he was able to unite his followers and obtain for them freedom from British domination. He fought with love and meekness rather than with violence, hatred, retribution, and revenge.

Job was meek, the epitome of strength. He taught that "the Lord gave, and the Lord hath taken away; blessed be the name of the Lord." (Job 1:21.)

The meekness of Mary, the mother of Jesus, has provided a source of strength to women through all generations. When the angel appeared to her and told her that the child she would bear would be called the Son of God, and that with God,

37

nothing is impossible, she replied, "Behold the handmaid of the Lord; be it unto me according to thy word." (Luke 1:38.)

Paul was meek — and bold, fearless, and strong. When Jesus appeared to him on the road to Damascus, he said, "Lord, what wilt thou have me to do?" (Acts 9:6.)

Returning to my account of the Argentine horses and the modern use in Spanish of the word *manso,* meaning a combination of being well trained and obedient, I would like to share two stories from my own experience or observations that emphasize the importance of obedience.

1. *Polo ponies.* It is important that horses used on the polo field be obedient. One way to select those horses is to first train the ponies to come to the trainer when he blows his whistle and to reward them for their obedience with kindness, affection, and sugar, carrots, or some other goodie. Then, after the whole group is trained to this point, the trainer will leave them all day in the corral without water. Water will be in a trough just beyond the corral gate, where the thirsty horses can see and smell it. At the end of the long, hot, dry day, the trainer will open the gate, and the horses will rush toward the trough. But just before they reach it, he will blow his whistle, signaling for them to return to him in the corral. The horses that are obedient will immediately stop, wheel around, and return to him, while those that are less obedient will satisfy their thirst before they return. These last horses, of course, will not be chosen.

2. *The test pilot.* When I was in the navy, one of my instructors told about an experience he had had as a test pilot for an airplane factory in the early days of World War II. He was asked to test a model that was important both to the factory, which needed to make the sale to the navy, and to the navy, which needed a plane that could perform better in combat than the enemy aircraft. The factory owners and engineers and admirals and other officers of the navy watched

intently as he took off and made his test flight; everyone gathered around the plane when he taxied up to the flight line and shut the engine down.

The pilot climbed down from the cockpit with his notes and commented, "As you observed, the plane got off in the minimum distance as marked by the flags." Everyone nodded; the distance represented the length of an aircraft carrier. Then he reported on the time it took to climb to 30,000 feet, explaining, "This ship climbs like a homesick angel. It is even better than the estimates and much better than the required minimums. At 30,000 feet, full throttle, second stage supercharger and water injection, she exceeded the projections by forty knots, a full 10 percent. She is like a bullet." Everyone smiled and nodded, looking very pleased. "In the power dive," he went on, referring to his notes, "I reached the red line of maximum design speed, inadvertently exceeded it slightly, and made an 8-G pullout. The wings, as you can see, did not bend nor break."

By this time the people were ready to celebrate — but then the test pilot dropped the bad news. "But unfortunately she is not ready for combat. I tried the required combat maneuvers — a loop, a chandelle, a snap roll, a tight turn at high speed — but *she just does not obey the controls.* She will go fast and straight, she will climb, but she will not maneuver. The engineers will have to make bigger control surfaces — change the ailerons, rudder, and elevator — so she will crank around faster, so she will be obedient. She is like a mule that does not want to change direction."

Oh, how important is the principle of obedience, even when one is dealing with animals and machines!

Another example is found in the Old Testament, where we are told that Naaman, a Syrian general, came down with the dreaded disease of leprosy. A Jewish servant convinced him that the prophet Elisha could heal him, so Naaman took his entourage across deserts, mountains, and plains to the place where the prophet lived. He sent his servant in to see, and the prophet sent back instructions that the general should go to the River Jordan and bathe seven times.

Naaman apparently expected a major miracle, with thunder, lightning, and perhaps an earthquake thrown in for effect, for his disappointment and misunderstanding of the ways of God are reflected in his question as to whether the rivers in Damascus were not better than all the waters of Israel: "May I not wash in them, and be clean?" And then, we are told, "he turned and went away in a rage." Fortunately the servant prevailed upon him to reconsider, and Naaman finally followed Elisha's instruction. According to the biblical report, "Then went he down, and dipped himself seven times in Jordan, according to the saying of the man of God: and his flesh came again like unto the flesh of a little child, and he was clean." (See 2 Kings 5:1–14.)

How often do we want a particular blessing and expect it to happen in our preconceived way rather than proceeding in obedience and faith? We can learn from Naaman's experience: when he finally did as he was instructed, he was blessed.

The old law taught that people should give "an eye for an eye, and a tooth for a tooth." The Savior gave a new, much higher law with no retribution and no revenge. He said, "Resist not evil: but whosoever shall smite thee on thy right cheek, turn to him the other also. And if any man will sue thee at the law, and take away thy coat, let him have thy cloke also." (Matthew 5:38–42.)

The attitude of revenge is completely counterproductive. It creates a vicious cycle: If you break off my tooth, then, so help me, I will break off your tooth! If carried to the extreme, such retribution can escalate and stretch out to infinity and even lead to a spirit of destruction. This is apparently the attitude that the wicked reached in the time of Mormon's last battle. Only when someone is strong enough, through meekness, to break this chain can the spirit of retaliation stop. By refusing to seek revenge, those who are meek stimulate peace within themselves and in society in general, a peace that can lead to the survival of individuals and of nations.

Meekness means finding a way to resist with love, not fighting with hatred. The person who is meek does not respond to frustration with revenge; he senses that revenge is a poison to his own spirituality, a cancer which can destroy him. Revenge tends to keep the wounds open which will only enlarge. One philosopher has said that meekness is like water that, when it meets an obstacle, rises slowly and patiently and ultimately runs over the obstruction and wears it away and conquers in the end.

Only meek, Christlike love can heal and turn the tide so that self-control and self-discipline can conquer anger, hatred, and revenge. Meekness is self-mastery, and therein lies the strongest element of this virtue.

CHAPTER 4

Blessed Are They
Who Hunger and Thirst

Book of Mormon: *"Blessed are all they who do hunger and thirst after righteousness [who come unto Christ], for they shall be filled with the Holy Ghost."* (3 Nephi 12:6.)

King James Version: *"Blessed are they which do hunger and thirst after righteousness: for they shall be filled."* (Matthew 5:6.)

Jerusalem Bible: *"Happy those who hunger and thirst for what is right: they shall be satisfied."*

Phillips Modern English Bible: *"Happy are those who are hungry and thirsty for true goodness, for they will be fully satisfied!"*

How many people strive for higher spiritual levels as though they truly hungered and thirsted after them? To hunger and thirst for something involves strife, struggles, work, sacrifice, and a host of other efforts.

As a young man, my father-in-law crossed a sixty-mile stretch of desert — with the temperature 118 degrees Fahrenheit in the shade! — on horseback with a limited supply of water. He had planned to meet a wagon train midway to replenish his water supply. Unbeknown to him, the wagon train had been unexpectedly delayed. When his water ran out, his dog died, his horse keeled over, and his tongue swelled horribly inside his mouth. He managed to survive, staggering out of the desert during the night. But as he told the story I could feel his intense, agonizing desperation for moisture. He truly thirsted.

Perhaps you have heard the story of the philosopher who held a young disciple's head under water until the latter gasped for air. The philosopher then told the disciple, "When you want knowledge as much as you wanted air while you were under water, you are ready to study with me."

The highest blessings of the gospel are not for the faint-hearted, coolly rational, theoretical philosopher, nor for the person who is merely intellectually curious. Those great blessings are reserved for stouthearted souls who hunger and thirst for greater personal righteousness and who are willing to pay the price to achieve it.

One need not have reached spiritual perfection or saint-hood to receive the blessings promised in this beatitude. If we sincerely hunger and thirst, the door to higher stairs will be opened, and we can climb them upward. The blessings are not so much in the arriving as in the constant seeking for perfection.

The blessings promised are immeasurable. Remember the woman of Samaria at the well? The Savior told her (and this applies to all of us), "Whosoever drinketh of the water that I shall give him shall never thirst; but the water that I shall give him shall be in him a well of water springing up into everlasting life.

"He that cometh to me shall never hunger; and he that believeth on me shall never thirst." (John 4:14; 6:35.)

The pathway to perfection is long and narrow, but each step brings rewards and hope and surety of even greater satisfying of spiritual hunger and thirst in the future.

The King James translation of this parable ends with the phrase "for they shall be filled." The Book of Mormon and the Joseph Smith Translation end with a much more reassuring declaration: "for they shall be filled with the Holy Ghost."

Filled with the Holy Ghost. What a marvelous promise! Just as a starving man craves food, and as my dehydrated father-in-law thirsted for water, so do the righteous yearn for the Holy Ghost as a constant companion. The Holy Ghost is a revelator, a testifier, a sanctifier; he reveals, and he cleanses men's souls. The Holy Ghost is the very spirit of truth, and his is the promised baptism by fire. The gift of the Holy Ghost is the greatest of all the gifts of God to man, as pertaining to this life; and those who merit that blessing here in mortality will inherit eternal life in the hereafter.

When we hunger and thirst to come unto the Savior, and hunger and thirst to achieve his righteousness, we are led to seek the companionship of the Saints, to gather on the Sabbath, and to enjoy worship, the sacrament, hymns of praise, and the brotherhood of our fellow members. This hunger and thirst of the spirit stimulates fervent and sincere prayers, fasting, good works, and sacrifice, and our desire to go to the temple increases. These lasting joys are more to be sought after than the fleeting pleasures of the world.

Why is it that some people seem to continue as spiritual children while others progress toward a noticeable spiritual maturity? Is it because of individual personalities? Is it because of some special spiritual experiences that one has been deprived of? Is it because of sin or lack of interest?

Why are some transformed and others not? Is it because the great change of heart or awakening out of a deep sleep spoken of by Alma (see Alma 5:7) is dependent upon our spiritual appetite, our spiritual desires? Is it because spiritual maturity is based upon our initiative? Should we seek and ask rather than waiting for something to happen?

Something seems to happen to those with voracious appetites for spiritual matters. They seem to receive greater fulfillment from reading the scriptures, attending gospel-oriented meetings, and serving others. Spiritual growth, spiritual maturity, and spiritual well-being are based upon and interdependent with spiritual appetite.

As a child, I was taught to read the scriptures, pray, and obey my parents. But I still remember the miracle of spiritual awakening prompted by the discovery of the book *Articles of Faith* by Elder James E. Talmage. It had long been in our modest library of Church books, but I had never noticed it. Then one day, looking for something to read, I pulled this book off the shelf. I must have been about twelve or thirteen at the time. As I skimmed through the chapters and noticed the marvelous depth of information assembled to support each one of the familiar and memorized Articles of Faith (memorized, thanks to a diligent Primary teacher), I felt a new, exciting spiritual appetite. I could not stop reading that fascinating book. I did not understand all the words, but that did not matter. I did not even stop to look up the unfamiliar words in a dictionary. What delighted me was the satisfying of my young mind for an organized, simple enlargement of the Articles of Faith, which I had committed to memory. I developed an appetite for reading about spiritual truths, an appetite that I have never lost.

Many prophets that we read about in the scriptures exhibit a great hunger and thirst for spiritual knowledge. They are curious and interested to the very core. Think of the appetite for spiritual knowledge that Nephi had, or Enos, or Jacob. Moses and Abraham wanted to know everything pertaining to God. Joseph Smith was blessed with an insatiable appetite for knowledge. David eloquently wrote: "As the hart [deer] panteth after the water brooks, so panteth my soul after thee, O God." Imagine the deer who is chased by the hunter until its thirst is excruciating, and it drinks quickly at the brook. David's psalm continues: "My soul thirsteth for God, for the living God: when shall I come and appear before God?" (Psalm 42:1–2.)

Sadly, occasionally we meet a person who once thirsted and hungered for spiritual things and then lost that appetite and turned to other interests. The loss of spirituality is immediately noticeable. I have known of missionaries who became distracted with things of the world — obsessed with the opposite sex, with watching TV or sports events — and who subsequently lost their appetite for spiritual things in a very short time and almost lost the spirit of their mission. What a tragedy! We must keep our eye single to the glory of God and look toward spiritual truths, or we too will lose our hunger and thirst for Christ and his righteousness.

One of the most important facts about this spiritual appetite is that it must come from within — it must result from our initiative. The saying "You can lead a horse to water but you cannot make him drink" is valid indeed. You can expose people to all sorts of spiritual experiences or scriptures or situations, but unless they have a deep desire or appetite that needs to be satisfied within themselves, it is all to no avail. For this reason spirituality is always self-motivated. If the hunger and thirst are not there, no one else can help us much. Unless we want to come unto Christ, no one can push us there.

What a tremendous addition is found in this beatitude as it is recorded in the Book of Mormon: Those who hunger and thirst after righteousness shall not just be filled, but they shall be filled *with the Holy Ghost!*

Through the gift of the Holy Ghost, the believer or disciple can cast out devils, speak with tongues, take up serpents, lay hands on the sick and they shall recover, receive the gift of knowledge, receive the gift of wisdom, and work miracles.

President B. H. Roberts, that great student of the gospel, wrote, "Such are the effects of the operations of the Holy Ghost upon the nature of man. These fruits of the Spirit indicate the change that the Spirit of God may effect in human nature; by which that which is corrupted through sin may be conformed to that which is pure and holy, according to the working whereby the Spirit is able to subdue all things unto Himself, in them that give place for his indwelling in their souls. This effectual working of the Spirit in the souls of men, by which they were transformed from vileness to holiness, was the boast of the early saints. And upon reflection all will concede that the victories of the Spirit in reforming the lives of men and making them in their very nature conform to the likeness of Christ in righteousness, are more to be desired and more to be celebrated than those victories which are physical or intellectual merely in their nature. Indeed these latter fruits of the Spirit derive their chief value from the extent to which they contribute to the production of the former—that is, to the extent that they establish men in the faith, enable them to crucify the flesh with the lusts thereof, and help them to live in harmony with the sweet influence of the Spirit of God. When men live in harmony with that Spirit there will righteousness obtain; there will love abound; there will the Gospel of Christ appear triumphant. Where these fruits do not appear, there the Gospel of Christ is not; there the powers of darkness for the time being, are triumphant." (*The Seventy's Course in Theology*, p. 189.)

The following is a partial list of the functions of the Holy Ghost:

The Holy Ghost teaches. (Luke 12:12.)

The Holy Ghost comforts. (John 14:16–17, 26.)

The Holy Ghost witnesses. (Acts 5:32.)

The Holy Ghost guides. (John 16:13–14.)

The Holy Ghost directs the calling of new leaders. (Acts 13:2, 4.)

The Holy Ghost reveals. (1 Corinthians 12:3.)

The Holy Ghost gives joy. (1 Thessalonians 1:5–6.)

47

The Holy Ghost gives understanding of the scriptures. (2 Peter 1:20–21.)

The Holy Ghost is the source of love for all men. (Romans 5:5.)

The Holy Ghost gives hope. (Romans 15:13.)

The Holy Ghost helps us pray. (Romans 8:26–27.)

John the Baptist had the authority to baptize by immersion, but he did not have the additional authority to baptize by fire or give the gift of the Holy Ghost.

Jesus gave this gift to the Twelve and to the Seventy he sent out to preach. This fact of two needed authorities is demonstrated in the story in Acts 8:15–17 of Philip preaching in Samaria. After he had baptized many at Samaria, the apostles at Jerusalem heard about his missionary success and immediately sent the apostles Peter and John to complete the work. They prayed for the new converts, who had not yet received the Holy Ghost, and then laid their hands on them. At that point the converts received the Holy Ghost. Acts 19:1–6 tells a similar story of Paul at Ephesus conferring the Holy Ghost after some new converts had been baptized. At that time it was apparently common for missionaries to baptize and then for brethren with higher authority to come along later and bestow the Holy Ghost by the laying on of hands. Today we know that the ordinance of baptism can be performed by those who hold the office of priest in the Aaronic Priesthood and that the gift of the Holy Ghost can be conferred only by those who hold the Melchizedek Priesthood.

How can we determine if someone "hungers and thirsts after righteousness"? One very simple way for a leader to learn if a member of the Church has this quality is if the person has a sincere desire to go to the temple, the house of the Lord. The experience we can have there is the highest spiritual experience we can enjoy on this earth. It is a truly celestial experience.

In the temple we can set our course on the eternities and learn how close we are to the straight and narrow path. We can go through the process of repentance and recommitment and review our overall level of spirituality and our relationship with our Heavenly Father and our family. In the temple, we determine if we have drifted from the iron rod and how much we need to correct our course to get back to where we should be.

It is interesting to note that to the Prophet Joseph Smith, the temple ordinances were so important and essential that in all his life he neither planned nor built a chapel — he only planned and built temples. He did not build a chapel in Kirtland, Ohio, but he built a temple. He did not plan a chapel in Independence, Missouri, but he planned a temple. He did not build a chapel in Nauvoo, Illinois, but he built a temple. He would not be indifferent toward going frequently to the house of the Lord. He had a tremendous hunger and thirst and drive to provide temples for the worthy Saints of this dispensation.

A Latter-day Saint who is not interested in the temple, who is not willing to make sacrifices to become worthy to go to the temple, and who is not striving to return to the temple probably will not come forth in the morning of the first resurrection. The well-established qualifications for the morning of the first resurrection are to be endowed in the temple and to remain worthy of a temple recommend to the end.

This certainly does not mean that those who have been to the temple should feel that they are any better than anyone else. It just means that there are certain, specific requirements listed in the scriptures, and they include the temple ordinances.

Elder Dallin H. Oaks has said that we cannot come unto Christ and be perfected in him without the covenants and ordinances of the temple. Moreover, the blessings of the gospel cannot be extended to our departed ancestors without the ordinances and covenants of the temple. Elder Boyd K. Packer has said that if we have received our covenants and ordinances, it does not matter what we might have missed in life. We can be ill, we can be afflicted, we can be poor, we can be ignorant of much of everything; but if we have received our ordinances, made our temple covenants, and kept those covenants, we have lived well. However, if we do not have those, whatever else we may have achieved in mortality will be of little appreciable value eternally.

A person who truly hungers and thirsts after righteousness wants to go to the temple. A temple is "a mountain of the Lord." Moses went to the mountain to commune with God. The ancients thought mountains and temples were places where contact was made between the spirit world and the temporal world; they also thought that temples and mountains were places where the gods passed from time to time from their celestial habitations to earthly residences. Those who truly hunger and thirst after righteousness want to climb that holy mountain often and pass that sacred test to fill themselves as one fills an empty vessel. Let us fill our vessels in the house of the Lord.

Another important test is the degree of hunger and thirst a person has to serve a mission for the Lord, truly one of life's greatest spiritual experiences. Today there is a greater urgency than ever before for members of the Church to prepare themselves to serve missions.

One scripture seems to indicate that the Savior considers that serving a mission, bringing souls to him, is a greater blessing than being at his holy feet in heaven. In 1829 Joseph Smith and Oliver Cowdery asked the Lord whether John, the beloved disciple, had tarried in the flesh or had died. In response, they received a translated version of a record made by John himself: "The Lord said unto me: John, my beloved, what desirest thou? . . . And I said unto him: Lord, give unto me power over death, that I may live and bring souls unto thee. And the Lord said unto me: Verily, verily, I say unto thee, because thou desirest this thou shalt tarry until I come in my glory, and shalt prophesy before nations, kindreds, tongues and people."

Peter, who had asked that he might quickly go unto the Lord in his kingdom, apparently questioned John's request, for we read that the Lord told Peter, "My beloved has desired that he might do more, or a greater work yet among men than what he has before done. Yea, he has undertaken a greater work." (D&C 7:1–6.)

In addition to going to the temple regularly and serving a mission worthily, there are other tests that clearly indicate the degree to which an individual hungers and thirsts after righteousness. Each of us might ask ourselves: How much desire do I have to live the gospel? How intent am I to consecrate myself to the Lord and his commandments and covenants? How strong is my desire to enjoy that mighty change of heart of which Alma taught? How close am I to the straight and narrow path, and am I making daily position checks to see if I need to change course in order to arrive at the right destination?

This is, ultimately, a very personal, private matter, and this beatitude should provoke great introspection by each person desiring to put his life in order and with proper priorities.

CHAPTER 5

Blessed Are the Merciful

Book of Mormon: *"Blessed are the merciful [who come unto me], for they shall obtain mercy."* (3 Nephi 12:7.)

King James Version: *"Blessed are the merciful: for they shall obtain mercy."* (Matthew 5:7.)

Jerusalem Bible: *"Happy the merciful; they shall have mercy shown them."*

Phillips Modern English Bible: *"Happy are the merciful, for they will have mercy shown to them!"*

"Our salvation rests upon the mercy we show to others. Unkind and cruel words, or wanton acts of cruelty toward man or beast, even though in seeming retaliation, disqualify the perpetrator in his claims for mercy when he has need of mercy in the day of judgment before earthly or heavenly tribunals. Is there one who has never been wounded by the slander of another whom he thought to be his friend? Do you remember the struggle you had to refrain from retribution? Blessed are all you who are merciful, for you shall obtain mercy!" (Harold B. Lee, *Stand Ye in Holy Places*, p. 346.)

When we think of mercy, we usually think of the relationship between justice and mercy. We all want the Lord to judge us with mercy. The Old Testament is full of references to the mercy we hope God will show toward us, both now and at the Day of Judgment. In this beatitude, the Savior talks

52

about our showing mercy in order to obtain mercy from God. The principle is that we will be judged with the same measure that we apply to others. This message is found in the parable of the unforgiving servant, where the king forgave the head servant who owed him ten thousand talents, but that same servant would not forgive his fellow servant who owed him only one hundred pence. The king, upon finding this out, declared: "O thou wicked servant, I forgave thee all that debt, because thou desiredst me: shouldest not thou also have had compassion on thy fellowservant, even as I had pity on thee?" (Matthew 18:32–33.)

The quality of mercy tempers the strict, severe sentence with compassion and an understanding of extenuating circumstances. The infinite mercy of God cancels any punishment if the sinner repents, asks for forgiveness, and promises to follow Christ. God's mercy comes from his unlimited and unconditional love for us. Likewise, we should show mercy to others through unlimited and unconditional love for them.

Our parents love us—not necessarily because we deserve it, but because they are our parents and we are their children. And because of their love, they sacrifice to provide for our welfare and security and happiness. Our Savior, Jesus Christ, loves us—not because we deserve it necessarily, but because we are his brothers and sisters. And because of his love, which is unconditional, the Savior willingly sacrificed his life for us. Sacrifice and service beget love.

The more we sacrifice for and serve others, the more we love them and forgive them their weaknesses, and the greater our tendency to extend mercy to them. When we don't love our family members or friends, we may think it is because they have not earned our love. But it is the other way around: if we do not love someone as much as we should, it is because we have not yet sacrificed enough for that person. That is why homes "blessed" with a parent suffering from an incurable disease or with a handicapped child are often so full of love.

Some years ago, while on a stake conference assignment in Idaho, I stayed in the home of a stake president who had a child afflicted with Down's syndrome. The child, who was about ten or twelve years old, was very full of unconditional love, and I was impressed with the relationship between that child and each one of the family members. On Sunday afternoon after the stake conference, I enjoyed a dinner with the families of the stake presidency and was surprised to note that each of those three families had a Down's syndrome child. I mentioned the coincidence to the stake president as he drove me to the airport to catch my plane home. He explained that the addition of their Down's syndrome child to his family had been a great blessing. Each member of the family had to make adjustments and sacrifices in order to take care of the handicapped one. To their surprise, the effect was that all of the children became softer and sweeter and more tender among themselves and toward parents and all others. He said, "That baby was a gift of God to our family, and we will never be the way we were before." Then he added, "When I was called as a stake president I looked around for the two most spiritual and loving men I could find. They, too, had Down's syndrome children. It seems that taking care of a child who needs more than the usual amount of attention increases love not only toward that child but toward everyone else as well. In our case it has not been a sacrifice but a great blessing."

"God so loved the world, that he gave his only begotten Son." (John 3:16.) Jesus so loved the world that he gave his life for us and suffered for our sins. Oh, what love! What mercy! Can we not find the way to be merciful to all those about us?

Elder Bruce R. McConkie wrote, "Mercy is for the merciful. In that great day of restoration and judgment, when every man is rewarded according to the deeds done in the flesh, those who have manifest mercy to their fellowmen here will be treated mercifully by the Merciful One. Those who have acquired the godly attribute of mercy here shall have mercy restored unto them again in that bright day." (*The Mortal Messiah* 2:122–23.)

In the Church we have a great army numbering in the hundreds of thousands or more of those we call "the less active members" or the "inactives," or those who are "careless about attending meetings." Bishops, stake presidencies, quorum leaders, and auxiliary leaders are exerting a major effort to try to reach out and invite them back. Some of those whom we are trying to bring into full activity have been offended. We can do little to correct the original wrongs, but if we can get the offended ones to forgive and forget and return, we will be blessed and they themselves will be blessed much more. The injunction by the First Presidency is that we encourage Church members to forgive those who may have wronged them. The Savior prayed, "Forgive us our debts, as we forgive our debtors." Then he counseled, "If ye forgive men their trespasses, your heavenly Father will also forgive you: but if ye forgive not men their trespasses, neither will your Father forgive your trespasses." (Matthew 6:12, 14–15.)

Returning to the parable concerning the unforgiving servant, perhaps we should go into a little more detail. The king's servant owed the king a considerable sum, ten thousand talents, which debt the king forgave out of compassion. But the same servant did not forgive his companion the small amount of a hundred pence, which was virtually insignificant. In *Jesus the Christ,* Elder James E. Talmage suggests that ten thousand talents would have amounted to millions of dollars in U. S. currency, while a hundred pence amounted to just a few dollars. When the king became aware of the level of injustice practiced by his servant, he, of course, had the servant jailed, or as some translators say, "delivered unto his tormentors." The punishment was decreed not because of the debt but because of the lack of mercy after having received mercy. The scriptures are clear: there is no mercy for those who do not show mercy.

Even if we have been offended or hurt or caused to suffer in any way, we must still forgive if we expect or hope that the Lord will overlook our weaknesses and sins, for can we say that there is even one of us without sin except Jesus himself?

When we forgive others, great things happen to us. A heavy burden is lifted from our backs, which then frees us to soar to higher spiritual levels. Take mercy away and we become very self-centered and empty. A person wrapped up in himself makes a very small package indeed. Some people may think that they are self-sufficient and that their salvation depends entirely upon themselves and no one else. It would appear from the examples we have cited thus far that this is not the case. Unless we have stepped outside ourselves and shown mercy to others who may not even deserve it, we ourselves cannot expect any mercy at the judgment bar.

Christ appears to have gone about the countryside of Judea looking for circumstances where he could demonstrate mercy as an example for us today. His gospel is very pertinent to our day and circumstances. He sought out the sick and the sinful and healed them of their bodily illnesses and their illnesses of the spirit. Even a woman taken in the act of adultery brought forth an unusual demonstration of mercy as he turned away her persecutors and then told her, "Neither do I condemn thee: go, and sin no more." (John 8:11.) In his love and healing, and through his association with the dreaded lepers, he showed mercy—even to the ones society had marked as untouchables or unacceptables.

In Shakespeare's *The Merchant of Venice*, Portia says to Shylock:

The quality of mercy is not strained,
It droppeth as the gentle rain from heaven
Upon the place beneath. It is twice blest;
It blesseth him that gives and him that takes.
'Tis mightiest in the mightiest. It becomes
The throned monarch better than his crown.
His scepter shows the force of temporal power,
The attribute to awe and majesty
Wherein doth sit the dread and fear of kings.
But mercy is above this sceptered sway,
It is enthroned in the hearts of kings,
It is an attribute to God himself,
And earthly power doth then show likest God's
When mercy seasons justice. Therefore, Jew,
Though justice be thy plea, consider this,
That in the course of justice none of us
Should see salvation. We do pray for mercy,
And that same prayer doth teach us all to render
The deeds of mercy.
— Act 4, scene 1

A touching story about mercy is told about President Abraham Lincoln. During the Civil War a young soldier fell asleep while on guard. The enemy took advantage of the weakness in the defense and attacked, killing many of the guard's fellow soldiers, and in the counterattack, more were killed. The guard, who survived and admitted his guilt, was court-martialed and, in keeping with wartime discipline, sentenced to death. He did not ask for mercy, but his mother did. She wrote a letter to President Lincoln and told him that at the beginning of the war she had a husband and four fine sons. Now her husband and three sons were all dead, due to the war. She pleaded not for her son but for compassion and mercy for herself because of all she had given. It is recorded that President Lincoln pardoned the young soldier and sent him home to take care of his mother — and no one criticized him for this act.

As a banker in South America, I had a personal experience that illustrates mercy and justice. I had made a loan to a man who exported lumber from the rain forests of Paraguay, transporting it downriver to Argentina. Then the river dropped to the lowest level in fifty years, making export impossible, so even though he had the logs, he could not ship and collect to pay off the loan. I renewed the loan for another six months and increased my security by taking a mortgage on all his property plus chattel mortgages on his tractors, trucks, and other logging equipment. When the loan came due the next time, the river was up but the market was low, and he didn't make enough profit to repay the loan. Again I agreed to renew the loan, since he had given me more than sufficient collateral. When the note came due this time, there was a revolution in Argentina and no buyers for his logs. But this time auditors were coming to the bank and, knowing that the loan would be classified (a black mark against me as a banker), I had to collect.

When I advised the man that I would have to legally take some of his property or equipment and sell it at forced sale to cover the loan, he pleaded for mercy. I explained justice. He demanded mercy. I demanded justice. It was a most tragic situation.

In the middle of this crisis my client's brother came to the bank to see me. He was also a client, with a large cattle ranch and a business in the capital city. He said, "If I pay my brother's loan, will you leave him alone?" I said that I would and that I would pass the mortgages to him. As for my part, justice had been satisfied with the payment, no matter where it came from.

In like manner, Christ has intervened between each of us and justice, paying with his sacrifice the debts that we owe.

However, this is conditional upon our having faith in him, repenting of our sins, being baptized, receiving the Holy Ghost by the laying on of hands, and continuing faithful to the end, which means obeying all his commandments, especially preparing for the covenants of the temple. Then and only then can the full measure of his atonement be available to us. Therefore, we must understand that the atoning sacrifice of Christ is real, but it is conditional upon our love of and obedience to him.

The New Testament has a few illuminating verses about the atonement of Christ, but the clearest scriptures explaining how it truly works are in the Book of Mormon. Following are a few of the most significant scriptures; additional ones may be found in the Topical Guide in the LDS edition of the King James Version of the Bible under the headings "Blood," "Fall of Man," "Forgiveness," "Jesus Christ, Atonement through," "Jesus Christ, Mission of," "Jesus Christ, Redeemer," "Jesus Christ, Savior," "Reconciliation," "Redemption," and "Sacrifice."

> Wherefore, redemption cometh in and through the Holy Messiah; for he is full of grace and truth. Behold he offereth himself a sacrifice for sin, to answer the ends of the law, unto all those who have a broken heart and a contrite spirit; and unto none else can the ends of the law be answered. Wherefore, how great the importance to make those things known unto the inhabitants of the earth, that they may know that there is no flesh that can dwell in the presence of God, save it be through the merits, and mercy, and grace of the Holy Messiah, who layeth down his life according to the flesh, and taketh it again by the power of the Spirit, that he may bring to pass the resurrection of the dead, being the first that should rise. Wherefore, he is the firstfruits unto God, inasmuch as he shall make intercession for all the children of men; and they that believe in him shall be saved. (2 Nephi 2:6–9.)

And he cometh into the world that he may save all men if they will hearken unto his voice; for behold, he suffereth the pains of all men, yea, the pains of every living creature, both men, women, and children, who belong to the family of Adam. . . . And he commandeth all men that they must repent, and be baptized in his name, having perfect faith in the Holy One of Israel, or they cannot be saved in the kingdom of God. . . . For the atonement satisfieth the demands of his justice upon all those who have not the law given to them, that they are delivered from that awful monster, death and hell, and the devil, and the lake of fire and brimstone, which is endless torment; and they are restored to that God who gave them breath, which is the Holy One of Israel. (2 Nephi 9:21, 23, 26.)

And thus God breaketh the bands of death, having gained the victory over death; giving the Son power to make intercession for the children of men — having ascended into heaven, having the bowels of mercy; being filled with compassion towards the children of men; standing betwixt them and justice; having broken the bands of death, taken upon himself their iniquity and their transgressions, having redeemed them, and satisfied the demands of justice. (Mosiah 15:8–9.)

And he shall come into the world to redeem his people; and he shall take upon him the transgressions of those who believe on his name; and these are they that shall have eternal life, and salvation cometh to none else. Therefore the wicked remain as though there had been no redemption made, except it be the loosing of the bands of death; for behold, the day cometh that all shall rise from the dead and stand before God, and be judged according to their works. (Alma 11:40–41.)

Therefore, according to justice, the plan of redemption could not be brought about, only on conditions of repentance of men in this probationary state, yea, this preparatory state; for except it were for these conditions, mercy could not take effect except it should destroy the work of justice. Now the work of justice could not be destroyed; if so, God would cease to be God.

And thus we see that all mankind were fallen, and they were in the grasp of justice; yea, the justice of God, which consigned them forever to be cut off from his presence.

And now, the plan of mercy could not be brought about except an atonement should be made; therefore God himself atoneth for the sins of the world, to bring about the plan of mercy, to appease the demands of justice, that God might be a perfect, just God, and a merciful God also. . . .

And if there was no law given, if men sinned what could justice do, or mercy either, for they would have no claim upon the creature?

But there is a law given, and a punishment affixed, and a repentance granted; which repentance, mercy claimeth; otherwise, justice claimeth the creature and executeth the law, and the law inflicteth the punishment; if not so, the works of justice would be destroyed, and God would cease to be God.

But God ceaseth not to be God, and mercy claimeth the penitent, and mercy cometh because of the atonement; and the atonement bringeth to pass the resurrection of the dead; and the resurrection of the dead bringeth back men into the presence of God; and thus they are restored into his presence, to be judged according to their works, according to the law and justice.

For behold, justice exerciseth all his demands, and also mercy claimeth all which is her own; and thus, none but the truly penitent are saved.

What, do ye suppose that mercy can rob justice? I say unto you, Nay; not one whit. If so, God would cease to be God. (Alma 42:13–15, 21–25.)

The heart and soul of all Christianity is the atonement of Christ and his sacrifice of his own free will to pay for our sins. There are two ways to look at the mechanics of the atonement. Of course, they are both speculation, since even the most competent of scholars and the most spiritual of leaders confess that no one knows how the Lord performs this miracle of miracles of paying for our sins. One approach uses a mathematical equation, saying that the infinite greatness of the Savior's sacrifice is so overwhelmingly magnificent that it totals more than the sum of the sins of all mankind, with an infinite balance left over. The second explanation is that the Savior's sacrifice is such that it entitles him to intervene on our behalf and ask for compassion, just as the mother in the Civil War story intervened and asked for compassion because of her sacrifice. Pondering details of the atonement may be good for our spiritual maturity as long as we increase every day our personal gratitude, love, and appreciation of the Savior and our determination to be worthy of his intervention on our behalf.

The words of this great sacrament hymn are worthy of memorization and daily repetition:

> I stand all amazed at the love Jesus offers me,
> Confused at the grace that so fully he proffers me.
> I tremble to know that for me he was crucified,
> That for me, a sinner, he suffered, he bled and died.
>
> I marvel that he would descend from his throne divine
> To rescue a soul so rebellious and proud as mine,
> That he should extend his great love unto such as I,
> Sufficient to own, to redeem, and to justify.
>
> I think of his hands pierced and bleeding to pay the debt!
> Such mercy, such love, and devotion can I forget?
> No, no, I will praise and adore at the mercy seat,
> Until at the glorified throne I kneel at his feet.
>
> Oh, it is wonderful that he should care for me
> Enough to die for me!
> Oh, it is wonderful, wonderful to me!
> —*Hymns,* no. 193

The greatest need for mercy is from God toward us. The next greatest need for mercy is from one human being toward his neighbor. The parable of the good Samaritan is the finest in the scriptures for demonstrating this principle. In fact, the Christian character or attitude is based upon generosity toward our fellowmen, leading us to make sacrifices for them just as Christ made an infinite sacrifice for us. The brotherly love and concern as demonstrated in that parable should be the guiding principle in our daily relationships with all those about us.

"A certain man went down from Jerusalem to Jericho, and fell among thieves, which stripped him of his raiment, and wounded him, and departed, leaving him half dead. And by chance there came down a certain priest that way: and when he saw him, he passed by on the other side. And likewise a Levite, when he was at the place, came and looked on him, and passed by on the other side.

"But a certain Samaritan, as he journeyed, came where he was: and when he saw him, he had compassion on him, and went to him, and bound up his wounds, pouring in oil and wine, and set him on his own beast, and brought him to an inn, and took care of him. And on the morrow when he departed, he took out two pence, and gave them to the host, and said unto him, Take care of him; and whatsoever thou spendest more, when I come again, I will repay thee.

"Which now of these three, thinkest thou, was neighbour unto him that fell among the thieves? And he said, He that shewed mercy on him. Then said Jesus unto him, Go, and do thou likewise." (Luke 10:30-37.)

Those who are merciful are full of the love of Christ, and show that Christlike love toward every person around them and with whom they have contact. Mercy, love, and charity are so interrelated that it is appropriate here to paraphrase that great declaration by Paul on charity, defined as the pure love of Christ, but substituting the word *mercy* for *charity*:

"Though I speak with the tongues of men and of angels, and have not mercy, I am become as sounding brass, or a tinkling cymbal. And though I have the gift of prophecy, and understand all mysteries, and all knowledge; and though I have all faith, so that I could remove mountains, and have not mercy, I am nothing. And though I bestow all my goods to feed the poor, and though I give my body to be burned, and have not mercy, it profiteth me nothing. Mercy suffereth long, and is kind; mercy envieth not." (1 Corinthians 13:1–4.)

The mercy of God is referred to approximately 150 times in the Old Testament. Students of the translation of the Old Testament point out that sometimes the original word *chesedh* is translated "mercy," and sometimes it is translated "goodness." The most common interpretation relates it to reducing the severity of the justice one deserves. But the alternate interpretation relates it to something that we also look forward to: that is, that the Lord, in his goodness of heart, loves us and has special blessings for us even in our imperfections. Both interpretations point to what we should show to our fellowmen, mercy and goodness — or, as the angel said in announcing to the shepherds the birth of the Savior, "On earth peace, good will toward men." (Luke 2:14.)

In Old Testament references, the concept of mercy is not negative; it is the willingness to hold justice in abeyance, to reduce a punishment, to mitigate the severity of that which is just and deserved. It is another facet of the love of God the Father to his children and the love of our Savior, King, and Redeemer toward us whom he has saved if we follow him, take his name upon us, testify of him, and remember and obey him — the promises of the sacrament prayers.

The promise of Christ's mercy is certain and available to

each one of us. He who turned water to wine, stilled the winds with his hand, walked on water, and performed myriad other miracles can also effect the miracle of personal peace for the sinner, the sufferer, the one who has erred and harmed others. His peace is made available to all of us because of his mercy toward us. He said, "Peace, be still," and also, "These things I have spoken unto you, that in me ye might have peace. In the world ye shall have tribulation: but be of good cheer; I have overcome the world." (John 16:33.)

Paul said it well: "Let us therefore come boldly unto the throne of grace, that we may obtain mercy, and find grace to help in time of need." (Hebrews 4:16.)

CHAPTER 6

Blessed Are the Pure in Heart

Book of Mormon: *"Blessed are all the pure in heart [who come unto Christ], for they shall see God."* (3 Nephi 12:8.)

King James Version: *"Blessed are the pure in heart: for they shall see God."* (Matthew 5:8.)

Jerusalem Bible: *"Happy the pure in heart: they shall see God."*

Phillips Modern English Bible: *"Happy are the utterly sincere, for they will see God!"*

To really understand this beatitude, we need to know what is meant by "pure in heart" and what is meant by seeing God. To be pure, a person's heart must be sincere and untainted by ulterior motives, conflicts of interest, or spiritually degrading influences.

Elsewhere in the scriptures we find promises similar to the statement "for they shall see God," and we believe that each of us can have our own dreams, visions, and manifestations in which we see God. Referring to this promise, Elder Bruce R. McConkie wrote the following:

"How glorious is the voice we hear from him! Man may see his Maker! Did not Abraham, Isaac, and Jacob see the Lord? Did not Moses and Aaron, Nadab and Abihu, and seventy of the elders of Israel see the God of Israel, under whose feet was a paved work of a sapphire stone? Was it not thus with Isaiah and Nephi, with Jacob and Moroni, and with mighty prophets without number in all ages? Is God a respecter of persons who will appear to one righteous person and withhold his face from another person of like spiritual stature? Is he not the same yesterday, today, and forever, dealing the same with all people, considering that all souls are equally precious in his sight? Did not Moses seek diligently to sanctify his people, while they were yet in the wilderness, that they might see the face of God and live? Does not the scripture say that the brother of Jared had such a perfect knowledge of God that he could not be kept from seeing within the veil? Why then should not the Lord Jesus invite all men to be as the prophets, to purify themselves so as to see the face of the Lord?

"It is written: 'Verily, thus saith the Lord: It shall come to pass that every soul who forsaketh his sins and cometh unto me, and calleth on my name, and obeyeth my voice, and keepeth my commandments, shall see my face and know that I am.' (D&C 93:1.) How glorious the concept is! What a wondrous reality! The pure in heart—all the pure in heart— shall see God!" (*The Mortal Messiah* 2:123.)

It makes little difference whether the seeing of God is physical or spiritual. The important part is that we commit ourselves to a course of purification and sanctification that will lead us to God, remembering always that after we have done all we can do, Christ is really the one who, through his atoning sacrifice, makes us clean before our Heavenly Father.

In the Spanish scriptures, the word *pure* is translated *limpios,* which means clean. It refers to ceremonial cleanliness, such as the emotions felt after baptism or performing the temple ordinances. Other interpretations refer to being clean of guilt, clean of bad habits, and clean of pollution.

In the original Greek text, the word *katharos* is used. The meaning is closer to clean than pure, and the word is used both to describe ceremonial purity or cleanliness and to de-

scribe moral and spiritual purity and cleanliness. The word
katharos is close to *catharsis*, which means a purging of all
impurity. (Another form of translation shows this Greek word
being used to describe thoroughbred lineage or unmixed racial
lineage, or a language free of slang, or a man free of debts.)

In English, we tend to use the words *clean* and *pure* somewhat interchangeably, as do the Greeks, with *pure* carrying a
definite moral and spiritual tone that implies integrity, innocence, and righteousness. It behooves us to understand both
of these uses. A spiritual discipline comes from obeying certain
rituals, ordinances, and covenants that involve ceremony, but
a spiritual awakening comes from the way of life we live, our
conduct, our thoughts, and the intents of our heart.

While in ancient Israel ceremonial purity might come from
washing one's hands with the fingers pointed upward till the
water flowed down to the wrists — or from the high priest bathing
his body in clean water five times and his hands and feet ten
times — members of Christ's church today tend to think of
being cleansed by the holy waters of baptism, which symbolically washes away our sins; by repenting so as to be worthy
of taking the sacrament weekly; or by preparing ourselves to
go to the temple to take part in ceremonies that purify and
cleanse us. But these are still all a form of physical washings
and anointings.

Jesus brought a new and higher law, adding to the old in
some cases and replacing the old in others. He brought to us
the concept of being pure and clean of heart, which is internal.
This is by far a greater law. This seems to be a matter of one's
heart, mind, and soul being free from impure thoughts and
attitudes. As members of Christ's church, we might say that
it is not enough to just be baptized or to have a temple recommend. A higher level of introspection is needed if we are
to be truly free from impurities. We might ask if we have truly
made that mighty change of heart spoken of by Alma:

"Have ye spiritually been born of God? . . . Have ye experienced this mighty change in your hearts? . . . Can ye imagine yourselves brought before the tribunal of God with your souls filled with guilt and remorse? . . . Can ye look up to God at that day with a pure heart and clean hands? . . . For there can no man be saved except his garments are washed white; yea, his garments must be purified until they are cleansed from all stain, through the blood of him of whom it has been spoken by our fathers, who should come to redeem his people from their sins." (Alma 5:12–21.)

In the Old Testament David asked similar questions: "Who shall ascend unto the hill of the Lord? or who shall stand in his holy place?" In the Church today, we might say: Who is worthy to go to the temple, which is the mountain of the Lord? Then David explained, "He that hath clean hands, and a pure heart; who hath not lifted up his soul unto vanity, nor sworn deceitfully. He shall receive the blessing from the Lord, and righteousness from the God of his salvation." (Psalm 24:3–5.)

In order that we have clean hands and a pure heart, it is obvious that our actions, our words, and our thoughts must be clean. Alma warns that "our words will condemn us, yea, all our works will condemn us; . . . and our thoughts [negative thoughts, improper thoughts, impure thoughts] will also condemn us." (Alma 12:14.)

A tendency to not be completely pure and clean, or hypocrisy, will catch up with us. If we do some good deed to be seen of men rather than to help the needy, if we sacrifice something in order to receive personal satisfaction, if our motive to go on a mission is more to learn a language or to see far-away places rather than to serve the Lord, if we seek a church position in order to receive honors of men instead of to humbly serve the Lord, we may not be found to have the pure hearts and clean hands that are needed in order to receive the blessings. A penetrating self-review, then, is necessary to avoid being condemned for what may appear at first glance to be worthy deeds. For example, some may preach against sexual sin with such detail that they could be found guilty of voyeurism or vicarious pornography.

Every day, in all that we say, do, or think, we are either approaching closer to the standards of the Savior or we are departing from them. To seek daily to have ever cleaner hands and a purer heart should be our goal. This requires that our emotions, desires, ambitions, motives, and innermost feelings be focused on Christ. With his help, we can repent and try to make some progress every day.

One of the strongest interpretations for being "pure in heart" has to do with sexual virtue and purity. We are told to "let virtue garnish [our] thoughts unceasingly." (D&C 121:45.) Sexual impurity is rampant in today's world. It first attacks thoughts, then words, then actions. For this reason, the Lord and his servants warn us often and strenuously against pornographic material. No one who is involved with such staining, tarnishing, corrosive, degenerating influences can be clean and pure.

From the time of Adam and down through and after the time of Moses, we hear the God of Israel strictly prohibiting such moral sins as fornication, adultery, homosexuality, and incest. At one time anciently these sins were punished by death. When the Savior was on earth, he changed the severity of that punishment, telling the woman taken in adultery to "go, and sin no more." Nevertheless, the sin is still so serious in the sight of the Lord that the prophet Alma told his son Corianton that sexual sins were second only to the shedding of innocent blood.

Today The Church of Jesus Christ of Latter-day Saints teaches that there is a single standard for both men and women: both should arrive at the sacred altar of marriage virgin and pure. We also teach that there should be no sexual relationship of any kind outside of marriage. Christ said, "Ye have heard that it was said by them of old time, Thou shalt not commit adultery: but I say unto you, That whosoever looketh on a woman to lust after her hath committed adultery with her already in his heart." (Matthew 5:27-28.) Today the Lord would perhaps phrase this commandment a little differently. To include today's sins he would have to say, "Whatever man or woman looketh on the opposite sex — or whatever man or woman looketh on the same sex — with lust in his (or her) heart has committed adultery with them in his (or her) own heart." We are unequivocally against sexual sins, which seem to be increasingly prevalent in our society, and we place a large part of the blame on the pornography and other suggestive material in the media, including television, movies, advertising, magazines, and books.

In the Book of Mormon reference to this beatitude, "Blessed are the pure in heart," we might add the phrase "who come unto Christ" to support the thought that no one can truly come unto Christ without passing through the process of faith in Christ, repentance of sin, and baptism for the remission of sins, followed by the laying on of hands for the gift of the Holy Ghost. Baptism is the key ordinance here, a requirement that cannot be changed or modified. Baptism by immersion is essential, and it must be performed by one who holds the legal authority to perform the ordinance, using the sacred prayer revealed by God in the beginning. The ordinance will then be binding both on earth and in heaven, and it must be recorded here and there. Just being pure in heart is not enough. We all must pass through the ceremonial purification process of becoming prepared for baptism and then going down into the water just as Christ did two thousand years ago as an example to us and to "fulfill all righteousness." He declared, "He that entereth not by the door into the sheepfold, but

climbeth up some other way, the same is a thief and a robber."
(John 10:1.)

This ordinance is essential for all who would seek entrance
into the kingdom of God, including those who have died
without having been baptized as well as those who were never
baptized in an authorized manner. The provision for baptism
by proxy, or baptism for and in behalf of those who are dead,
existed in the ancient Christian church and it exists in the
restored church of Jesus Christ today. Of course, the earthly
ordinance is not valid unless those on the other side of the
veil are prepared for and accept the ordinance done for them
here. Nevertheless, we have the sacred duty to research our
ancestors and do these required Christian ordinances for them.
Paul, in his epistle to the saints at Corinth, asked, "Else what
shall they do which are baptized for the dead, if the dead rise
not at all? why are they then baptized for the dead?" (1 Corinthians 15:29.)

While we do not have a full or detailed explanation of
baptism for the dead in ancient times, it is evident that members of the early church did perform the ordinance. Many
references to this practice in ancient literature, in addition to
those found in the Bible, have been discovered in recent times.
Professor Hugh Nibley of Brigham Young University, one of
the Church's finest authorities on this subject, has studied an
impressive number of ancient documents and sources that
support the concept that while Christ did not say anything
on the subject during his earthly ministry, he taught the doctrine of baptism for the dead and other temple ordinances
during the forty days he spent with the apostles after his resurrection and before his ascension. After his ascension, the
apostles taught the doctrine to selected leaders but were careful
not to leave written instructions. Just as today we consider
the temple ordinances and covenants for the dead to be so
sacred that we do not talk about them in detail, so in their

day the apostles had the same instructions. Dr. Nibley writes: "In 1895 there was found in Egypt a Coptic papyrus purporting to contain an account of the teaching of Christ to his apostles after the resurrection. The most learned church historian of modern times, Adolf von Harnack, was prompted to point out that this document was neither 'a provincial production of the Egyptian Church' nor a brainchild of the Gnostics, but an authentic statement of certain important doctrines of salvation and resurrection common to the whole Christian church at a very early date." (*Mormonism and Early Christianity,* volume 4 in the Collected Works of Hugh Nibley, p. 100.)

An analogy about being pure in heart can be learned from an experience our family had when we lived in South America. A storm with high velocity winds struck a wooded area near our home, blowing down an unusually large number of trees. Upon inspection, it was found that a new species of worm had attacked the hearts of the trees, weakening them. From the outside they appeared to be healthy with bark intact, but at the center they were rotten. In order to withstand the winds of adversity, one needs to be pure in heart (having the core free from rotting), which requires obedience to the laws, ordinances, covenants, doctrines, and policies of the kingdom of God on earth.

The Savior used strong language in an allegory to teach this principle: "Woe unto you, scribes and Pharisees, hypocrites! for ye are like unto whited sepulchres, which indeed appear beautiful outward, but are within full of dead men's bones, and of all uncleanness. Even so ye also outwardly appear righteous unto men, but within ye are full of hypocrisy and iniquity." (Matthew 23:27–28.)

In Isaiah and in the Doctrine and Covenants, we find the same command: "Be ye clean, that bear the vessels of the Lord." (Isaiah 52:11; see also D&C 38:42.)

Paul wrote to the saints at Corinth: "What? know ye not

that your body is the temple of the Holy Ghost which is in you, which ye have of God, and ye are not your own? For ye are bought with a price: therefore glorify God in your body, and in your spirit, which are God's." (1 Corinthians 6:19–20.)

In Alma we read: "He [God] doth not dwell in unholy temples; neither can filthiness or anything which is unclean be received into the kingdom of God; therefore I say unto you the time shall come, yea, and it shall be at the last day, that he who is filthy shall remain in his filthiness." (Alma 7:21.)

Moroni counseled, "Be wise in the days of your probation; strip yourselves of all uncleanness; ask not, that ye may consume it on your lusts, but ask with a firmness unshaken, that ye will yield to no temptation, but that ye will serve the true and living God." (Mormon 9:28.)

The Lord, through the Prophet Joseph Smith, commanded us: "I give unto you, who are the first laborers in this last kingdom, a commandment that you assemble yourselves together, and organize yourselves, and prepare yourselves, and sanctify yourselves; yea, purify your hearts, and cleanse your hands . . . before me, that I may make you clean." (D&C 88:74.)

The promise attached to this impressive beatitude is that the pure in heart will see God. President Harold B. Lee declared: "If you would see God, you must be pure. There is in Jewish writings the story of a man who saw an object in the distance, an object that he thought was a beast. As it drew nearer he could perceive it was a man; as it came still closer he saw it was his friend. You can see only that which you have eyes to see. Some of the associates of Jesus saw Him only as a son of Joseph the carpenter. Others thought Him to be a winebibber or a drunkard because of His words. Still others thought He was possessed of devils. Only the righteous saw Him as the Son of God. Only if you are the pure in heart will you see God, and also in a lesser degree will you be able to see the 'God' or good in man and love him because of the goodness you see in him. Mark well that person who criticizes and maligns the man of God or the Lord's anointed leaders in His Church. Such a one speaks from an impure heart." (*Stand Ye in Holy Places*, p. 345.)

President Marion G. Romney said: "Jesus spoke of specific rewards for different virtues but reserved the greatest, so it seems to me, for the pure in heart, 'for they,' said he, 'shall see God' (Matt. 5:8). And not only shall they see the Lord, but they shall feel at home in his presence. Here is his promise — the Savior's promise: 'Let virtue garnish thy thoughts unceasingly; then shall thy confidence wax strong in the presence of God' (D&C 121:45).

"The rewards for virtue . . . are dramatically portrayed in the [life] of Joseph. . . . Joseph, though a slave in Egypt, stood true under pressure of the greatest temptation [when Potiphar's wife tried to seduce him]. As a reward [for resisting] he received the choicest blessings of all the sons of Jacob: he became the progenitor of the two favored tribes of Israel. Most of us take pride in being numbered among his posterity." (Conference Report, April 1979, p. 60.)

Whether or not we see God depends upon our spiritual level of maturity. When the Savior appeared at the temple in the land Bountiful, a group of twenty-five hundred men, women, and children had gathered, people who because of their righteousness had survived the destruction. Yet some did not understand when the Father spoke the first time, nor did they understand when he spoke the second time. We read: "The third time they did hear the voice, and did open their ears to hear it; and their eyes were towards the sound thereof; and they did look steadfastly towards heaven, from whence the sound came. . . . The third time they did understand the voice which they heard; . . . and behold, they saw a Man

[Christ] descending out of heaven; and he was clothed in a white robe; and he came down and stood in the midst of them." (See 3 Nephi 11:3–8.)

A parallel event in the Gospel of John illustrates the same point, although it has to do with hearing God instead of seeing him. When Jesus prayed to his Heavenly Father, "Father, [I] glorify thy name," the Father answered from heaven. Some of those who stood nearby said that it thundered, but others more tuned to the Spirit said, "An angel spake to him." (See John 12:28–29.)

The concept of actually seeing God in this life is a basic part of the doctrine of the Church. The Doctrine and Covenants has several references to this principle.

In section 88 the Lord tells us: "Therefore, sanctify yourselves that your minds become single to God, and the days will come that you shall see him; for he will unveil his face unto you, and it shall be in his own time, and in his own way, and according to his own will." (D&C 88:68.) In other words, no amount of our effort alone will bring about this miracle. It is a blessing bestowed upon the pure of heart after the trial of their faith. We cannot be seekers only; we must be doers and leave the timing of the miracle up to God.

In section 93 we read: "Verily, thus saith the Lord: It shall come to pass that every soul who forsaketh his sins and cometh unto me, and calleth on my name, and obeyeth my voice, and keepeth my commandments, shall see my face and know that I am." (D&C 93:1.) This is apparently not just a promise for the next life but an offering to the truly faithful while they are yet in mortality.

It must be admitted that there are two legitimate meanings to this matter — that of seeing God here in mortality and that of entering heaven and seeing him. Both include the same requirements of our becoming as nearly perfect as we can and then, through the process Jesus offers us, of his lifting us the rest of the way to perfection. His atonement paid the price for our imperfections, and we may be made perfect through him. He has told us: "These are they who are just men made perfect through Jesus the mediator of the new covenant, who wrought out this perfect atonement through the shedding of his own blood." (D&C 76:69.)

Some individuals have been allowed to see the face of God in this life. In Doctrine and Covenants 84 we read what is required for this to happen: "This greater priesthood [the Melchizedek Priesthood] administereth the gospel and holdeth the keys of the mysteries of the kingdom, even the key of the knowledge of God. Therefore, in the ordinances thereof, the power of godliness is manifest. And without the ordinances thereof, and the authority of the priesthood, the power of godliness is not manifest unto men in the flesh; for without this [priesthood] no man can see the face of God, even the Father, and live." (D&C 84:19–22.)

Adam, Moses, and other ancient prophets were blessed to see the face of God. We know that in our present dispensation, Joseph Smith saw both the Father and the Son; this is recorded in the story of the First Vision. (See Joseph Smith–History 1:17.) The Savior also appeared to the Prophet and to Oliver Cowdery in the Kirtland Temple. Joseph described this glorious vision:

"The veil was taken from our minds, and the eyes of our understanding were opened. We saw the Lord standing upon the breastwork of the pulpit, before us; and under his feet was a paved work of pure gold, in color like amber. His eyes were as a flame of fire; the hair of his head was white like the pure snow; his countenance shone above the brightness of the sun; and his voice was as the sound of the rushing of great waters, even the voice of Jehovah, saying: I am the first and the last; I am he who liveth, I am he who was slain; I am your advocate with the Father." (D&C 110:1–4.)

In the second epistle of Peter, three concepts are intro-
duced that relate to our discussion: (1) seeing the Son and/
or the Father; (2) receiving the Second Comforter; and (3)
making one's calling and election sure. The Prophet Joseph
Smith put these things in perspective. After discussing the
Holy Ghost, or first Comforter, he explained:

"The other Comforter spoken of is a subject of great interest, and perhaps understood by few of this generation. After
a person has faith in Christ, repents of his sins, and is baptized
for the remission of his sins and receives the Holy Ghost, (by
the laying on of hands), which is the first Comforter, then
let him continue to humble himself before God, hungering
and thirsting after righteousness, and living by every word of
God, and the Lord will soon say unto him, Son, thou shalt
be exalted. When the Lord has thoroughly proved him, and
finds that the man is determined to serve Him at all hazards,
then the man will find his calling and his election made sure,
then it will be his privilege to receive the other Comforter,
which the Lord hath promised the Saints, as is recorded in
the testimony of St. John, in the 14th chapter, from the 12th
to the 27th verses. . . .

"Now what is this other Comforter? It is no more nor less
than the Lord Jesus Christ Himself; and this is the sum and
substance of the whole matter; that when any man obtains
this last Comforter, he will have the personage of Jesus Christ
to attend him, or appear unto him from time to time, and
even He will manifest the Father unto him, and they will take
up their abode with him, and the visions of the heavens will
be opened unto him, and the Lord will teach him face to face,
and he may have a perfect knowledge of the mysteries of the
Kingdom of God; and this is the state and place the ancient
Saints arrived at when they had such glorious visions—Isaiah,
Ezekiel, John upon the Isle of Patmos, St. Paul in the three
heavens, and all the Saints who held communion with the

general assembly and Church of the Firstborn." (*Teachings of the Prophet Joseph Smith,* pp. 150–51.) As we strive to become true followers of Christ — inwardly as well as outwardly — we soon learn that the critical element is progress, not longevity. At the end of this life, the question will be how well we have lived and what progress we made toward perfection, not how long we lived.

Elder Dallin H. Oaks has said, "The issue is not what we have *done* but what we have *become.* And what we have become is the result of more than our actions. It is also the result of our attitudes, our motives, and our desires. Each of these is an ingredient of the pure heart. . . . To become pure in heart — to achieve exaltation — we must alter our attitudes and priorities to a condition of spirituality, we must control our thoughts, we must reform our motives, and we must perfect our desires." (*Pure in Heart,* pp. 139–40.)

Our ultimate reward will be as the Savior promised: "Blessed are the pure in heart: for they shall *see* God."

C H A P T E R   7

Blessed Are the Peacemakers

Book of Mormon: *"And blessed are all the peacemakers [who come unto Christ], for they shall be called the children of God."* (3 Nephi 12:9.)

King James Version: *"Blessed are the peacemakers, for they shall be called the children of God."* (Matthew 5:9.)

Jerusalem Bible: *"Happy the peacemakers: they shall be called the sons of God."*

Phillips Modern English Bible: *"Happy are those who make peace, for they will be known as sons of God!"*

In this beatitude, those who are blessed are not particularly those who love peace, but those who *make* peace. The blessed ones are those who are the "doers of the word," not just passive listeners. (See James 1:22.) Whether we say "those who make peace" or "peacemakers," it is the verb *make* that brings such power to this beatitude. In order to bring down the blessings of heaven, we must be actively making peace in the home, the office, the social groups we move in, the Church, the classroom, the neighborhood, the community, the world.

Two of our daughters studied in Israel with Brigham Young University's study-abroad program. In almost every letter they wrote home, they used the word *shalom*. We understood from them that *shalom* means peace and that it is used most often in two senses. The first is a greeting in which one wishes for the person addressed happiness and tranquillity. The second is as a term describing friendship and goodwill between two people.

The word *peace* appears almost a hundred times in the New Testament and seems always to be closely identified with Christ as the Prince of Peace. The Savior had no material wealth to give to others, but he frequently gave blessings of peace.

We long for peace as we look upon this war-torn world with its open strife, terrorism, and tension between nations. We honor statesmen and diplomats who are peacemakers. But the Savior was not talking about peace between nations achieved after a military victory, or through bilateral agreements worked out by the leaders of two nations, or through resolving strikes or disturbances within nations. Rather, he referred to the peace that comes to the heart of a person who lives the commandments; comes unto Christ with a broken heart and a contrite spirit, repenting and exercising faith; enters into the waters of baptism; and receives the peaceful, comforting Spirit of the Holy Ghost.

May I share with you a story I heard from an eyewitness to significant events that occurred during the Vietnam War. At the time the president and the congress of the United States were convinced that the U.S. was involved in a noble and justifiable war against communism. However, opposition among individuals in the media and in the public was escalating, with many arguing that the U.S. should pull out of the war. Those who favored continued fighting were called hawks, and those who opposed the war were called doves. In the midst of this divisive controversy, President Harold B. Lee became the president and prophet of The Church of Jesus Christ of Latter-day Saints. Shortly after he was set apart, he went to Mexico City for an area conference of the Church, and there the international press corps asked for interviews with him.

A press conference can always include questions intended to trap the person being interviewed, in order to provoke that person to give unexpected responses. The trap question newsmen planned to ask President Lee was "What is your position on the Vietnam War?" If he answered "We are against it," they could write "How strange—a Mormon leader who is against the position of the president and congress of his country." If he answered "We are in favor of it," they could print "How unusual—a Mormon leader who is in favor of war!" Either way, the answer could result in serious problems regarding public opinion, both inside and outside the Church.

When the question was posed to him, President Lee, with great inspiration and wisdom, answered as a true prophet would: "We, together with the whole Christian world, abhor war. The Savior said, 'In me ye might have peace. In the world ye shall have tribulation.' " And then he quoted that comforting scripture from John 14:27: " 'Peace I leave with you, my peace I give unto you: not as the world giveth, give I unto you. Let not your heart be troubled, neither let it be afraid.' " He explained, "The Savior was not talking about the peace that can be achieved between nations by military force or by negotiation in the halls of congress. Rather he was speaking of the peace we can each have in our own hearts when we live the commandments and come unto Christ with a broken heart and contrite spirit."

The members of the press were impressed with that undisputable response, and the resulting coverage of the interview was more accurate and favorable than almost any other similar interview members of the press had conducted.

Too many homes are torn by strife and tension between husband and wife, between parents and children, and between siblings. The home is the first and most important place to establish peace. Blessed is that person who makes peace happen in the home. This sought-for peace can come from different avenues, including praying for guidance, seeking professional counseling, listening to priesthood leaders, reading books written by accepted experts on family relationships and communication, being willing to change oneself, and making sacrifices for the sake of peace.

Elder Bruce R. McConkie wrote the following: "The gospel of peace makes men children of God! Christ came to bring peace — peace on earth and good will to men. His gospel gives peace in this world and eternal life in the world to come. He is the Prince of peace. How beautiful upon the mountains are the feet of them who preach the gospel of peace, who say unto Zion: Thy God reigneth! Let there be peace on earth, and let it begin with his saints. By this shall all men know the Lord's disciples: they are peacemakers; they seek to compose difficulties; they hate war and love peace; they invite all men to forsake evil, overcome the world, flee from avarice and greed, stand in holy places, and receive for themselves that peace which passeth understanding, that peace which comes only by the power of the Spirit. And these are they who are adopted into the family of God." (*The Mortal Messiah* 2:123–24.)

If peacemakers are going to be adopted into the inner family of God and be called the children of God, then it might follow that troublemakers, lawbreakers, those who disturb peace and order, leaders of ruthless mobs, and any who are prompted by evil intent or total selfishness, to the destroying of peace, will be known as children of Satan. Those who spread confusion, those who attack or criticize sacred things, and those who quarrel or argue or are of a contentious spirit all violate the spirit of this beatitude and are not creating peace and goodwill among men.

Can we imagine that in the heavens above and the life to come there will be anger, hate, jealousy, fighting, discord, shouting, egotism, selfishness, and so forth? Not at all! That would be a hell, not a heaven. This life is the place to learn how to get rid of every negative passion, every ornery tendency, that leads individuals to destroy peace in their environment. In this life we must learn how to turn to Christ and his ways and reject any temptation to follow Satan's ways of discord. Here we must learn how to create and to live in peace and harmony so we can be ready to live in the presence of Heavenly Father, his Son, Jesus Christ, and the prophets.

When the Savior came here to the American continent and found contention among the people, he warned them, "There shall be no disputations among you, as there have hitherto been. . . . He that hath the spirit of contention is not of me, but is of the devil, who . . . stirreth up the hearts of men to contend with anger, one with another." (3 Nephi 11:28–29.)

Later, repeating the sermon he had given on the mount in the Holy Land, he said that we should not ever become angry. That means that we should never raise our voices except to warn someone of impending danger, nor show any other negative, satanic passion. We are to develop and exhibit self-control — control of our voice, words, gestures, actions, and body language. Anger and lack of control are destructive to the spirit. The Spirit of Christ is reflected in the smile, warm tone of voice, happy expression, and peace in the demeanor of the true follower of the Prince of Peace.

Peace means unity and harmony. It is interesting that the Lord told members of the first quorums of leadership in the Church in this dispensation that every decision made by either quorum "must be by the unanimous voice of the same; that is, every member in each quorum must be agreed to its decisions," and that decisions were to be made "in all righteousness, in holiness, and lowliness of heart, meekness and long suffering, and in faith, and virtue, and knowledge, temperance, patience, godliness, brotherly kindness and charity."

(D&C 107:27, 30.) With all these spiritual qualities, there is an abundance of peace.

Zacharias, the father of John the Baptist, spoke regarding the role that the Savior would have. He said that Christ would "give light to them that sit in darkness and in the shadow of death, to guide our feet into the way of peace." (Luke 1:79.) The righteous always long for peace and tranquillity and look forward to that day when peace will cover the entire earth as a blanket. Until that day comes, the best hope we have is to create peace in our own hearts and in our own surroundings, no matter what is going on in the world.

The Savior said that in the world we would have tribulation, but in him we might have peace. He is our only solution. He is the only way and the only life. Everything always comes back to following Christ.

In 1947 the First Presidency issued the following statement: "Faith in God is the first essential to peace. It is folly for the United Nations now seeking ways and means to permanent peace to exclude the idea of God from their deliberations. Only through an acknowledgement of the Divine Being as Father can the sense of human brotherhood have potency. Only thus can life have purpose and humanity as a whole live in peace." (*Improvement Era,* January 1947, p. 13.)

In the Sermon on the Mount, when the Savior gave higher laws to replace the old laws, he replaced the custom of retribution with this new law: "Resist not evil: but whosoever shall smite thee on thy right cheek, turn to him the other also." (Matthew 5:39.) The peacemaker learns that a soft answer turns away wrath (see Proverbs 15:1), and that the ways of love and peace can and do produce miracles when the hearts of others are softened.

The Savior faced many trials and tribulations, but as an example to us he met every situation with peace. He declared: "Peace I leave with you, my peace I give unto you: not as the world giveth, give I [peace] unto you." (John 14:27.) We are told that if we will follow the strait and narrow path and come unto Christ, he will give us peace in the midst of difficulties. No matter the buffetings, the fiery darts, the mockings, the discouragements; if we will follow Christ, we will become the adopted children of Christ in a family of peace. (See Mosiah 5:7.)

One of the most excruciating and disturbing effects of sin is the absence of peace in the lives of those who sin. Sinners are tormented by their conscience. They suffer in agony, knowing how disappointed their Heavenly Father is with them. Alma, in telling his son Helaman about his own sins, confessed, "I went about with the sons of Mosiah, seeking to destroy the church of God." (Alma 36:6.) Then, Alma said, an angel visited him and reminded him of his sins. "I was struck with such great fear and amazement lest perhaps I should be destroyed," he explained. Then he really began to suffer. "I was racked with eternal torment, for my soul was harrowed up to the greatest degree. Yea, I did remember all my sins and iniquities, for which I was tormented with the pains of hell; yea, I saw that I had rebelled against my God, and that I had not kept his holy commandments. . . . And now, for three days and for three nights was I racked, even with the pains of a damned soul."

In the midst of his suffering, Alma remembered the teachings of his father about coming to Christ, and a miracle of peace occurred. He recounted this remarkable experience: "As my mind caught hold upon this thought, I cried within my heart: O Jesus, thou Son of God, have mercy on me. . . . And now, behold, when I thought this, I could remember my pains no more. Yea, I was harrowed up by the memory of my sins no more. And oh, what joy, and what marvelous light I did behold; yea, my soul was filled with joy as exceeding as was my pain!" (See Alma 36:6–20.) Through turning to Christ,

Alma was given peace of mind and heart. That is the miracle of the Atonement. When we truly turn to our Savior, he gives us peace. When we repent of our sins, they torment us no more.

The peace of the repentant sinner is relief, like the balm of Gilead. The gospel song says, "There is a balm of Gilead that heals the sin-sick soul." We all need that peace. The Savior used the sheep of the fields and hills as symbols of peace. The pastoral environment is one of the most peaceful that one can imagine. Even the story of the shepherd going to look for the lost sheep is full of joy and peace as the lost one is returned to the fold.

Paul talked of Christ "having made peace through the blood of his cross, by him to reconcile all things unto himself" (Colossians 1:20), by which we understand that the only way we can have true peace is also through his blood that was shed for us. If we come to him regularly through partaking of the sacrament, taking his name upon us, always remembering him, and always testifying of him, then we will have his peace with us.

Paul began each of his epistles with some reference to Christ's peace. He was sure that Christ was at peace with himself and with his Father, and that we each must be at peace with them also. In fact, missionary work is the work of bringing people to peace with Christ and God. Paul calls it reconciliation. In his second letter to the Corinthians he said, "God, who hath reconciled us to himself by Jesus Christ, . . . hath given to us the ministry of reconciliation." (2 Corinthians 5:18.) He then declared that we are ambassadors for Christ and that we should bring all people to be reconciled to God. Through missionary work, we bring people to the waters of baptism, and through baptism they receive remission of their sins and peace in Christ. There is no peace quite like that of a sacred baptismal service. To make peace with God is to promise to obey him and to follow Christ. A missionary is a peacemaker.

One of the ways to peace is through forgiving those who have offended us. So long as we feel offended, there can be no peace in our hearts. Feeling offended is a type of anger and resentment that poisons the spirit of peace and forces it out of our hearts. In the scriptures, we are taught to treat this malady through the miracle of forgiveness. The miracle is first up to us: we must forgive those who have offended us. The Lord has commanded: "Ye ought to forgive one another; for he that forgiveth not his brother his trespasses standeth condemned before the Lord; for there remaineth in him the greater sin." (D&C 64:9.) When we truly forgive others, we can have peace. Furthermore, when we forgive others the Lord forgives us. What a magnificent promise! The source of peace is found through forgiving and forgetting.

In the beatitudes Christ promises that peacemakers will become "children of God." In the Book of Mormon King Benjamin makes a statement in his temple sermon that has confused a few students of the scriptures. He says: "Because of the covenant which ye have made ye shall be called the children of Christ, his sons, and his daughters; for behold, this day he hath spiritually begotten you; for ye say that your hearts are changed through faith on his name; therefore, ye are born of him and have become his sons and his daughters." (Mosiah 5:7.)

The scriptures clearly state that we are all sons and daughters of our Heavenly Father. Christ is also a son of our Heavenly Father. He is our elder brother. We are all brothers and sisters of Christ and of each other. How then can we be sons and daughters of Christ?

Paul indicates that we are Christ's sons and daughters by adoption. Some kind of intimate bond, with a symbolic adoption by Christ, develops when we have made certain changes and certain covenants with him. Paul told the Ephesians that we have been "predestinated . . . unto the adoption of children by Jesus Christ to himself." (Ephesians 1:5.) To the Galatians Paul wrote that "God sent forth his Son . . . to redeem them that were under the law, that we might receive the adoption of sons." (Galatians 4:5.)

Truly, as we make peace in all the different facets of our lives, we can become the adopted children of Christ, our Lord, and come to enjoy his true peace, the peace of the Second Comforter.

CHAPTER 8

Blessed Are the Persecuted

Book of Mormon: *"Blessed are all they who are persecuted for my name's sake [who come unto me], for theirs is the kingdom of heaven."* (3 Nephi 12:10.)

King James Version: *"Blessed are they which are persecuted for righteousness' sake: for theirs is the kingdom of heaven."* (Matthew 5:10.)

Jerusalem Bible: *"Happy those who are persecuted in the cause of right: theirs is the kingdom of heaven."*

Phillips Modern English Bible: *"Happy are those who have suffered persecution for the cause of goodness, for the kingdom of Heaven is theirs!"*

How can persecution be a blessing? Since many who are persecuted die for their beliefs and faith in Christ, these blessings obviously are received in the next life rather than here; therefore, this beatitude is often referred to as the blessing of the martyrs. In the days of the New Testament, the words *witness* and *martyr* were virtually synonymous. Witnessing, or bearing testimony, has always brought persecution and turned the faithful into martyrs. Christ warned his followers that they would be persecuted. "Then said Jesus unto his disciples, If any man will come after me, let him deny himself, and take up his cross, and follow me. For whosoever will save his life shall lose it: and whosoever will lose his life for my sake shall find it." (Matthew 16:24–25.)

90

Few people have been persecuted more for their faith than was Paul, the apostle. He recounted some of his sufferings: "Are they ministers of Christ? (I speak as a fool) I am more; in labours more abundant, in stripes above measure, in prisons more frequent, in deaths oft. Of the Jews five times received I forty stripes save one. Thrice was I beaten with rods, once was I stoned, thrice I suffered shipwreck, a night and a day I have been in the deep; in journeyings often, in perils of waters, in perils of robbers, in perils by mine own countrymen, in perils by the heathen, in perils in the city, in perils in the wilderness, in perils in the sea, in perils among false brethren; in weariness and painfulness, in watchings often, in hunger and thirst, in fastings often, in cold and nakedness." (2 Corinthians 11:23–27.)

Paul was well aware that one who suffers persecution and tribulation for the noble cause of Christ becomes stronger spiritually. In his epistle to the Romans he wrote: "We glory in tribulations also: knowing that tribulation worketh patience; and patience, experience; and experience, hope." (Romans 5:3–4.)

Paul was not in jeopardy until he bore his testimony. He described his conversion: "As I made my journey, and was come nigh unto Damascus about noon, suddenly there shone from heaven a great light round about me. And I fell unto the ground, and heard a voice saying unto me, Saul, Saul, why persecutest thou me? And I answered, Who art thou, Lord? And he said unto me, I am Jesus of Nazareth, whom thou persecutest." The audience listened only a little bit more, their anger rising at his bold testimony, and then they started to shout, "Away with such a fellow from the earth: for it is not fit that he should live. And as they cried out, and cast off their clothes, [they] threw dust into the air." (Acts 22:6–8; 22–23.) All of this was a little ceremony used to show extreme provocation, somewhat like a bull pawing the dirt before charging. They would have killed him on the spot had he not appealed to the chief captain and the centurion for protection by virtue of his Roman citizenship.

In his second epistle to the Corinthians, Paul made a kind of understatement concerning his sufferings, but at the same time a beautiful testimony of his willingness to give all to the Savior: "We are troubled on every side, yet not distressed; we are perplexed, but not in despair; persecuted, but not forsaken; cast down, but not destroyed; always bearing about in the body the dying of the Lord Jesus, that the life also of Jesus might be made manifest in our body. For we which live are alway delivered unto death for Jesus' sake, that the life also of Jesus might be made manifest in our mortal flesh. . . . For which cause we faint not; but though our outward man perish, yet the inward man is renewed day by day. For our light affliction, which is but for a moment, worketh for us a far more exceeding and eternal weight of glory." (2 Corinthians 4:8–11, 16–17.)

Another dramatic example is Stephen, who could have continued preaching, as many pagans did, as a kind of entertainer in the central squares. Many philosophers, poets, and various religious fanatics did just that. But then Stephen looked up into heaven and saw a vision. "I see the heavens opened, and the Son of man standing on the right hand of God," he testified. And the people "cried out with a loud voice, and stopped their ears, and ran upon him with one accord, and cast him out of the city, and stoned him." (Acts 7:56–58.)

The Prophet Joseph Smith is a modern-day example of one who was persecuted for testifying that he had had a vision of the Father and the Son. He reported:

"Some few days after I had this vision, I happened to be in company with one of the Methodist preachers, who was very active in the before mentioned religious excitement; and, conversing with him on the subject of religion, I took occasion to give him an account of the vision which I had had. I was greatly surprised at his behavior; he treated my communication not only lightly, but with great contempt, saying it was all of the devil, that there were no such things as visions or revelations in these days; that all such things had ceased with the apostles, and that there would never be any more of them.

"I soon found, however, that my telling the story had excited a great deal of prejudice against me among professors of religion, and was the cause of great persecution, which continued to increase; and though I was an obscure boy, only between fourteen and fifteen years of age, and my circumstances in life such as to make a boy of no consequence in the world, yet men of high standing would take notice sufficient to excite the public mind against me, and create a bitter persecution; and this was common among all the sects—all united to persecute me.

"It caused me serious reflection then, and often has since, how very strange it was that an obscure boy, of a little over fourteen years of age, and one, too, who was doomed to the necessity of obtaining a scanty maintenance by his daily labor, should be thought a character of sufficient importance to attract the attention of the great ones of the most popular sects of the day, and in a manner to create in them a spirit of the most bitter persecution and reviling. But strange or not, so it was, and it was often the cause of great sorrow to myself.

"However, it was nevertheless a fact that I had beheld a vision. I have thought since, that I felt much like Paul, when he made his defense before King Agrippa, and related the account of the vision he had when he saw a light, and heard a voice; but still there were but few who believed him; some said he was dishonest, others said he was mad; and he was ridiculed and reviled. But all this did not destroy the reality of his vision. He had seen a vision, he knew he had, and all the persecution under heaven could not make it otherwise; and though they should persecute him unto death, yet he knew, and would know to his latest breath, that he had both seen a light and heard a voice speaking unto him, and all the world could not make him think or believe otherwise.

"So it was with me. I had actually seen a light, and in the midst of that light I saw two personages, and they did in reality speak to me; and though I was hated and persecuted for saying that I had seen a vision, yet it was true; and while they were persecuting me, reviling me, and speaking all manner of evil against me falsely for so saying, I was led to say in my heart: Why persecute me for telling the truth? I have actually seen a vision; and who am I that I can withstand God, or why does the world think to make me deny what I have actually seen? For I had seen a vision; I knew it, and I knew that God knew it, and I could not deny it, neither dared I do it; at least I knew that by so doing I would offend God, and come under condemnation." (Joseph Smith—History 1:21–25.)

During his short life the Prophet was cast into prison thirty-eight times, but not once was he found guilty of the crime of which he was accused. He was chased from state to state and seldom given any peace. He was beaten, tarred and feathered, left for dead, and finally murdered. I feel that he was not murdered so much for political or economic reasons as for bearing powerful testimony that he had seen the Father and the Son, for declaring: "I saw two Personages, whose brightness and glory defy all description, standing above me in the air. One of them spake unto me, calling me by name and said, pointing to the other—*This is My Beloved Son. Hear Him!*" (JS–H 1:17.)

The Savior was not crucified for giving the Sermon on the Mount, for walking on water, for healing the sick, or for any other miracle that he performed. Ultimately, he was condemned to death for testifying that he was the Son of God, the Messiah for whom all Israel had been waiting. When the high priest asked him, "Art thou the Christ, the Son of the Blessed?" he responded, "I am: and ye shall see the Son of man sitting on the right hand of power, and coming in the clouds of heaven. Then the high priest rent his clothes, and saith, What need we any further witnesses? Ye have heard the blasphemy: what think ye? And they all condemned him to be guilty of death." (Mark 14:61–64.) Jesus was persecuted and crucified because he testified of the truth. He truly is the Son of God.

It is perhaps inevitable that members of The Church of Jesus Christ of Latter-day Saints find themselves looked upon with suspicion by many. It was so in the early Christian dispensation. It was so in the early pioneer times of this dispensation. Today most people are well informed and look upon the Church and its members with respect, recognizing the good fruits of our unique way of life and the same Christian doctrines, covenants, and ordinances as existed in the days of Christ. However, the prophets have said that persecution will come again in the last days, although we do have the assurance that it will not destroy the Church. The righteous will be protected and the work will go forward, as Daniel of old prophesied.

The Prophet Joseph Smith gave us this promise: "The Standard of Truth has been erected; no unhallowed hand can stop the work from progressing; persecutions may rage, mobs may combine, armies may assemble, calumny may defame, but the truth of God will go forth boldly, nobly, and independent, till it has penetrated every continent, visited every clime, swept every country, and sounded in every ear, till the purposes of God shall be accomplished, and the Great Jehovah shall say the work is done." (*History of the Church* 4:540.)

Elder Bruce R. McConkie wrote about the role of persecution. He first quoted the following verses of scripture:

"Blessed are ye, when men shall hate you, and when they

95

shall separate you from their company, and shall reproach you, and cast out your name as evil, for the Son of man's sake. Rejoice ye in that day, and leap for joy: for, behold, your reward is great in heaven: for in the like manner did their fathers unto the prophets." (Luke 6:22.)

"Blessed are all they who are persecuted for my name's sake, for theirs is the kingdom of heaven. And blessed are ye when men shall revile you and persecute, and shall say all manner of evil against you falsely, for my sake; for ye shall have great joy and be exceedingly glad, for great shall be your reward in heaven; for so persecuted they the prophets who were before you." (3 Nephi 12:10–12.)

Commenting on these scriptures, Elder McConkie wrote: "How could it be said better? Jesus is speaking to the members of his earthly kingdom. In our day that kingdom is The Church of Jesus Christ of Latter-day Saints. It is composed of those who have taken upon them the name of Christ — covenanting in the waters of baptism to honor that name and to do nothing that will hold it up to contempt or ridicule. It is composed of those who have forsaken the world; who have crucified the old man of sin; who have become humble, meek, submissive, willing to conform to all that the Lord requires of them.

"And, of course, the world loves its own and hates the saints. The world is the carnal society created by evil men; it is made up of those who are carnal and sensual and devilish. Of course the world persecutes the saints; the very thing that makes them saints is their enmity toward the things of the world. Let the ungodly and the evildoers reproach the Lord's people; let them cry transgression against his saints; let persecution rage against those who bear the Lord's name; let true believers be reviled and evilly spoken of — all for his name's sake. So be it!

"Do they face trials of cruel mockings and scourgings? Are they stoned, sawn asunder, slain with the sword? Are they destitute, afflicted, tormented? Are they cast into dens of lions and furnaces of fire? Are they slain in gladiatorial arenas, lighted as torches on the walls of Rome, crucified head downward? Are they driven from Ohio to Missouri, and from Missouri to Illinois, and from Illinois to a desert wilderness — leaving their Prophet and Patriarch in martyrs' graves? No matter! They do not live for this life alone, and great shall be their reward in heaven." (*The Mortal Messiah* 2:124–25.)

President Harold B. Lee, speaking to the youth of the Church, made the following stirring comment: "May youth everywhere remember that warning when you are hissed and scoffed at because you refuse to compromise your standards of abstinence, honesty, and morality in order to win the applause of the crowd. If you stand firmly for the right, despite the jeers of the crowd or even physical violence, you shall be crowned with the blessedness of eternal joy. Who knows but that again in our day some of the saints or even apostles, as in former days, may be required to give their lives in defense of the truth. If that time should come, God grant they will not fail." (*Stand Ye in Holy Places,* pp. 347–48.)

Brother William E. Berrett wrote this about persecution: "Certainly the promise of membership in the kingdom has given courage to thousands who have faced persecution and death. Many did not seek persecution, they would have gladly escaped it. But faced with it — consumed by it — they rejoiced in the understanding that was given them by the Spirit because of baptism and the laying on of hands." (*Blessed Are They Who Come unto Me,* p. 90.)

The persecutions of the ancient Christians and of the early Saints of this dispensation might give us some idea why tomorrow's Saints might also be persecuted.

We are all familiar with the trials of today's converts who do not receive support from friends and family. Some are asked to leave home. Others are told they are not welcome at family gatherings because they are a source of embarrassment to other members of the family. Some are cut out of family wills and ostracized in many ways.

In business, members of the Church sometimes find that certain top positions are not open to them in spite of superior qualifications. In other, more severe cases the misguided employer severs them from the company when their religious nature is discovered. Such things are not the trend today, but they have happened.

Perhaps our future persecution will come from such things as our belief in the principles contained in the Word of Wisdom, or because of our stand against abortion. Maybe it will be due to a position that is taken to be political rather than spiritual, such as a position against gambling (including lotteries). Or perhaps persecution will come because men have always held the priesthood, according to the lineage of the fathers, and not women—although the Church has always been in favor of the full participation of women in church activities and ordinances. Or perhaps our missionaries will be persecuted and even murdered because the headquarters of the Church are in the United States.

As the world becomes more wicked, the polarization between God's ways and the world's ways will cause a gap that might lead to persecution of the followers of Christ.

It is easy to escape persecution: just follow popular opinion and the ways of the world; teach that salvation does not require strict adherence to Christ's commandments and covenants; make it easy to enter the celestial kingdom; make righteousness old-fashioned; downplay the importance of the scriptures and the teachings of the prophets.

The greatest defense against persecution, however, is to adhere to the principles of the gospel, to hold onto the iron rod. "Love your enemies, bless them that curse you, do good to them that hate you, and pray for them which despitefully use you, and persecute you." (Matthew 5:44.)

Joseph of Egypt was persecuted for being righteous and was thrown into a well. Miraculously, he was rescued from the well by the intervention of the Lord, and later he was freed from prison. By the hand of the Lord he ultimately became prime minister of Egypt. Daniel was thrown into the lions' den because he persisted in worshiping the God of Israel instead of worshiping King Darius. The Lord sent an angel to shut the lions' mouths, saving Daniel from harm, and he was restored to his former position of prominence — first leader under the king. The King James Version states that he was the first of three presidents set over a hundred and twenty princes, which position would be similar to that of prime minister.

All martyrs, and all who come unto Christ despite threats or realities of persecution, will find their due reward in the kingdom of heaven. Their treasure is where no one can steal or spoil it. Their salvation is assured.

C H A P T E R   9

The Salt of the Earth;
the Light of the World

Book of Mormon: *"Be the salt of the earth. . . . Be the light of this people. . . . Let your light so shine before this people, that they may see your good works and glorify your Father who is in heaven."* (3 Nephi 12:13.)

King James Version: *"Ye are the salt of the earth. . . . Ye are the light of the world. . . . Let your light so shine before men, that they may see your good works, and glorify your Father which is in heaven."* (Matthew 5:13-16.)

Jerusalem Bible: *"You are the salt of the earth . . . you are the light of the world. . . . Your light must shine in the sight of men, so that, seeing your good works, they may give the praise to your Father in heaven."*

Phillips Modern English Bible: *"You are the earth's salt. . . . You are the world's light. . . . Let your light shine . . . in the sight of men. Let them see the good things you do and praise your Father in Heaven."*

This section of the Sermon on the Mount is a major missionary scriptural commandment. It is significant that it comes close to the beginning of the Savior's first full recorded sermon. Missionary work was destined to be a significant part of the early Christian church under the direct guidance of the Savior. This went very much contrary to the philosophy of

Jewish leaders, even though Israel has had a missionary effort at times in her history.

While some authors believe that parts of the Sermon on the Mount were intended only for the apostles and that in a way this was their ordination sermon, it is also evident that the Savior intended for every follower of the Master to be a missionary and an example. Just as salt gives flavor to food to make it more palatable, so missionary success gives a new and better flavor to every church unit and to every town or city. Missionary effort and success are contagious and build spirituality and enthusiasm among individuals of every age and position in the Church. Nothing is quite so rewarding as missionary success. Likewise, stagnation, disappointment, and diminishing results in missionary efforts have the opposite result. The Lord reminds us that if the Saints "are not the saviors of men," or not doing missionary work up to their potential, "they are as salt that has lost its savor, and is thenceforth good for nothing." (D&C 103:10.) Woe be unto that leader or that unit or those members who have lost their missionary enthusiasm and have ceased to pray every day for missionary opportunities and have ceased to "open their mouths" at every chance.

In the same manner, the commandment to be a light to the world and not to hide one's light under a bushel is strong missionary counsel. To have "the right stuff" may be an overworked slogan in the flying and space world, but it is still something we have great need of in missionary work. We need the right missionary spirit, the right missionary zeal. We should be seeking at all times to be shining examples of the gospel, and in every aspect of life we should be living in righteousness, in keeping with the commandments of Jesus. We should be setting examples so that all who see us might be interested in what it is that brings such joy into our lives—the gospel of Jesus Christ. We live in a world full of temptations, with

Satan's influence increasing. We must resist his enticings so that we can be examples of Christ and the Christian ethic in every circumstance. We need to be ready to stand up and be counted on the issues that matter.

In the *Church News* dated February 18, 1989, readers responded to an invitation to share comments on being good member missionaries. Here are some of the responses:

"Being 'missionary-minded' means to look for opportunities to tell others about the gospel. When the opportunity arises, we must be prepared to talk to others about the Church. 'Role playing' in an imaginary situation can help prepare you about what to say to an interested friend or acquaintance. Use your ward mission leader as a resource. Call him for assistance. Have him come to your home for a family home evening and share ideas for getting started in missionary work. Also keep copies of the Book of Mormon at home, in the car and at work and give them away to someone showing interest." (John Boyle.)

"Sometimes adults feel they are not ready to attend Church, but they would like their children to have religious training. We can help teach these children the gospel by taking them to Primary. This involves more than giving them a ride. It may mean calling them on Saturday to remind them to be ready, helping them feel comfortable in their classes and being their special friend at Church. We do not see immediate results, but they are there. One member of our ward told how neighbors began bringing her and her brothers and sisters to Primary, although her parents were not Church members. As a result, more than 30 people in her family are active Church members today. She never fails to express her gratitude to the kind neighbors who shared with her family the blessings of the gospel." (Kathleen Hedberg.)

"Many of our best friends . . . were nonmembers that we invited to our home. There, they met other members of the

Church and saw the gospel in action. In our home, questions could be answered and information shared in a very natural way. When we felt the Spirit touch them, we would ask them to hear the missionary discussions. Most often they answered 'yes.' I recommend the following: cultivate nonmember friends; open your mouth and invite them to hear the discussions." (President and Sister V. Dallas Merrell.)

"Set a date, write it [down and put it] on your refrigerator and experience the joy of being a co-partner with God in bringing the gospel to nonmembers. In 1988 we rejoiced in four baptisms resulting in part from our set-a-date program. When we set a date, we tell the missionaries our date, pray earnestly on a daily basis and fast on fast day that Heavenly Father will lead us to someone, or someone will be led to us. Our answers always come. For example, a young couple asked us to discuss 'Mormonism' with them. A young man came to my husband's office and asked to be taught 'organized religion.' A student asked us about 'the young men who wear the black badges.' All were eventually baptized and are active." (June Christensen.)

President Harold B. Lee quoted many times the scripture in Doctrine and Covenants 88:67, both as written and in an opposite way, in the following manner: "If your eye be single to my glory," and he added parenthetically that the glory of the Lord is missionary work — bringing the children of men to immortality and eternal life, "your whole bodies shall be filled with light, and there shall be no darkness in you; and that body which is filled with light comprehendeth all things." Then he emphasized the opposite: "And if your eye *not* be single to my glory," and he repeated that missionary work is the glory of God, "then your whole bodies shall be filled with *darkness,* and there shall be no light in you; and that body which is filled with darkness does *not* comprehend anything." He added that those who are filled with darkness do not understand their leaders and frequently criticize them, moan and complain about things, and often disobey instructions and/or enter into apostasy.

There is a great division between those who really put their hearts and souls into missionary work and those who prefer to be uninvolved and leave it to someone else. They just never get the same light.

The scriptures are replete with missionary commandments. The following are a few examples that give an idea of the spirit of this noble work, carried out by commandment:

"Go ye therefore, and teach all nations, baptizing them." (Matthew 28:19.)

"Repentance . . . should be preached in his name among all nations." (Luke 24:47.)

"Go and bring forth fruit." (John 15:16.)

"Preach . . . repentance, and faith on the Lord Jesus Christ." (Alma 37:33.)

"The voice of warning shall be unto all people." (D&C 1:4.)

"Ye are called to bring to pass the gathering of mine elect." (D&C 29:7.)

"Feed my sheep." (John 21:17.)

"It shall be given unto such to bring thousands of souls to repentance." (Alma 26:22.)

"Thousands . . . do rejoice, and have been brought into the fold of God." (Alma 26:4.)

"The field was ripe, and . . . ye did thrust in the sickle, and did reap." (Alma 26:5.)

"How great will be your joy if you should bring many souls unto me!" (D&C 18:16.)

The whole core and intent of missionary work is to bring repentant souls unto Christ through faith, repentance, and baptism, and the other saving ordinances. The goal of being the salt of the earth and a light to the world is to bring souls to Christ, just as the scriptures declare.

A modern scripture, Doctrine and Covenants 7:1–7, has a unique missionary interpretation. As I understand the account, the Savior asked his apostles what was the desire of their hearts. Peter must have answered first, always eager and willing and perhaps somewhat impetuous, exclaiming that he desired that he might more speedily die and go unto Christ in His heavenly kingdom. By contrast, John the Beloved asked to be a missionary here on earth, saying, "Lord, give unto me power over death, that I may live and bring souls unto thee." The Savior, much impressed with John's response, turned to Peter and said, in effect: You want a good thing, but John has desired a greater thing. In other words, in the view of the Savior, it is greater to be a missionary on earth, bringing souls unto him, than to be in heaven worshiping at his feet. What a lesson for us!

The key to successful missionary work in Latin America, where my experience has been, is through working with the members. Full-time missionaries, when they work closely with members, produce remarkable results. I believe that the same techniques can be applied with minor adjustments anywhere in the world. The procedures are simple and time-tested — and very effective. Reduced to the simplest explanation, these are the procedures:

For each pair of full-time missionaries, members are asked to find about ten families who can be taught the gospel. Each pair of full-time missionaries should teach twenty or more discussions per week, with more than half of their investigators attending church every Sunday. Wherever possible, members would assist the missionaries as "junior companions," allowing the missionaries to "split" and thus meet more teaching appointments. Members are also asked, where possible, to bring the investigators to church services on Sundays. Members may also be asked to make regular visits to the investigators and provide other fellowshipping support.

Success comes when the full-time missionaries are so spiritually and mentally prepared that the members see them as veritable "angels." Moroni tells us that angels still minister to the children of men and that angels do the same things that missionaries do. (See Moroni 7:29–31.) Both angels and missionaries have an office of their ministry to (1) call people to repentance; (2) "do the work of the covenants of the Father," or bring people to the covenant of baptism; and (3) declare "the word of Christ unto the chosen vessels of the Lord," or the elect who have been prepared by the Spirit. Since ministering angels and full-time missionaries have the same commission, we may assume that spiritually oriented people feel the presence of angels as they come unto Christ and that they feel the same way toward missionaries.

Members of the Church may also share in the inspiration and joy that comes from association with the full-time "angel" missionaries through learning how to form effective proselyting habits. While missionaries have been called to give full-time service to their work, they may, through short visits, help members to become better trained and motivated in ways to assist with the missionary efforts. The Saints who help in this way should do so because of their love for the Lord and his work and not because of feelings of obligation. They can seek guidance through daily prayer and scripture study. In their private and family prayers they can ask the Lord to lead them to individuals and families whom they might approach.

The "golden questions" are a highly effective means to approach people in order to discover those who might be ready to receive the gospel. Simply ask: "How much do you know about my church, The Church of Jesus Christ of Latter-day Saints?" After listening carefully to their response, be it negative or positive, ask, with a prayer in your heart for the Lord's blessings, "Would you like to know more?" Then you might issue an invitation for them to come to your home to hear a presentation from representatives of the Church—the missionaries. We have found that it is more effective if the meeting with the missionaries is not combined with a dinner or other social activity for the investigators. A simple offer of juice and cookies after the missionaries leave following the discussion is more than enough social attention and will not detract from the discussion itself.

At one of my stake conference assignments, I learned about a member who had been successful in bringing three families into the Church that year. I asked how he found them. He told me of his family's daily prayers and custom of seeking for opportunities to ask the golden questions daily.

The first success was a family across the street. That husband left for work at exactly the same time as the member. In fact, they had to be careful that they did not back their cars into one another. One morning the neighbor's battery would not turn the motor over fast enough to start. Neither of the men had jumper cables. Since both were in a hurry to leave, the member offered the neighbor a ride to work and to pick him up to bring him home. During the drive, the member turned the conversation to his church meetings of the recent weekend. By the time he dropped the neighbor off at his office, he had asked the golden questions and set up a tentative appointment for him and his family to meet with the missionaries. On the way home that evening he was able to confirm the appointment. This neighbor family subsequently met with the missionaries, attended church services, and accepted baptism.

The second family lived a block or so away. The member did not have a telephone, so he would occasionally go to the neighbors' home to use theirs, and would always leave a Church tract or a small gift, such as homemade bread, cookies, or jam.

He also took occasion to ask the golden questions. One day the neighbors overheard a phone conversation in which the member was helping to make arrangements for a bereaved family. The next time the member asked the golden questions, the neighbor family, touched by the Spirit, responded in the affirmative. The member did not realize until much later that it was his example of church service that had impressed them. The neighbors were baptized.

The third family moved into a home over the back fence of the members. One evening before family home evening, the members' children were playing rather noisy games in their backyard and the neighbor children came out to watch. They were invited to join in the fun, which they did. When the parents came out to see what their children were doing, they were invited to join in the games. Then the members invited the neighbor family to stay for family home evening, which included scripture reading, musical numbers, a lesson, some refreshments, and a short parlor game. The neighbors were especially impressed by the closing prayer offered by one of the younger children while everyone knelt down. They wished that their children might be able to pray that well in the presence of guests. The member father asked the golden questions of his neighbor the next day and an appointment was set up. The discussions began in the members' home and were later moved to the neighbors' home. They were baptized.

Members who do not pray for missionary opportunities seldom have these kinds of experiences. It is a matter of changing habits and attitudes to fit the Lord's needs. If we do so, the Lord will bless us all.

Another simple way the members can do missionary work is through using and sharing the Book of Mormon. At a stake conference I felt prompted to call on a sister to bear her testimony. The stake president pointed out a woman in the audience whom he identified as the mother of a new bishop, and I asked for her to come forward. This is the story she told:

Her son and his family had joined the Church a few years before and then had tried to convert her. They gave her books, tracts, and magazines, and a couple of times they gave her copies of the Book of Mormon, which she did not read. Then just a few months before the stake conference, they gave her another copy of the Book of Mormon, this time gift-wrapped. She opened the gift and discovered a leather-bound, large-print book with gold edging and indexes and her name embossed in gold on the cover. Inside was a picture of her son and his family and a written testimony from them. She suspected that the book was expensive, so she decided to read just two pages so she could make an intelligent comment when thanking them. First she read the introduction and the testimonies of the three witnesses, the eight witnesses, and Joseph Smith. Then she went on to read the first two pages of First Nephi. When she phoned her son and thanked him for the gift, she remarked, "I have been reading the Book of Mormon and have read the introduction and the first two pages. Son, it's true, isn't it?" "Yes, Mother," he replied, "it is true." "Well . . . "—she paused—"I give up. Send the missionaries!" I saw both laughter and tears in the audience as she closed her lovely testimony.

Members of the Church who are anxious to share the joy that has come into their lives because of the gospel of Jesus Christ are truly the salt of the earth, a light to the world. Missionary work is exciting, the greatest spiritual adventure of all time. We just need to get involved.

One mistake that is frequently made is for members to wait too long to bring friends to church, to believe that the investigators need to be prepared first for however long it takes. This is counterproductive. In fact, a sacrament meeting service has great converting power itself. In one survey we found that as many as one-half of the friends brought to a sacrament meeting subsequently joined the Church. The key can be found in Doctrine and Covenants 84:20: "In the ordinances [of the gospel], the power of godliness is manifest." The most simple of services in the most humble of circumstances has converting power.

Forty years ago an elegant, sophisticated investigator went to church for the first time. Though the meeting was marked by some confusion and noise, she commented, "Don't apologize. It must have been like this at the time of Christ." She saw back through the centuries to a time when simple fishermen, probably smelling of fish, listened to the Savior in the open air by the shores of Galilee. It was the spirit of the meeting that had impressed her, and she was later baptized.

We need not hide that light which is the spirit of a sacrament meeting service. In time, every knee will bend and every tongue will confess that Jesus is the Christ, that this is his Church, and that they will want to come unto him.

Be that friend; be the salt that has its savor; be that light that will guide others to the light and eternal joy of the gospel.

Another aspect of this admonition of being the salt of the earth and a light to the world is that of simply, quietly living the principles of Christian service to others, apart from personal proselyting benefits. It means being an example of unselfish service like the good Samaritan.

The Latin American Lamanite people among whom we have lived are especially generous toward those in need. Whenever a friend, relative, or neighbor has a serious need, such as a place to sleep or food to eat, or in time of illness, they are given shelter, food, or are attended to, whatever the need is. It seems very natural for them to be "good Samaritans," taking people into their homes and sharing whatever of this world's possessions they have. It also seems that the less people have, the more willing they are to give to others. Some would say that this trait exists because they have so little and therefore it doesn't make much difference, but I have observed this for many years and have come to feel that it is more because those who are deep in poverty have suffered so much that they are more compassionate toward anyone else who has lost their home, their job, their money, their hope.

During times of general crisis, this attribute readily becomes apparent. A case in point was the earthquake in Mexico City in 1985 that left thousands homeless and destitute. Quickly they were accommodated in the homes of people close by. Those who decided to stay in their own area, living in tents, did so because that seemed more familiar to them and not because no one offered help. The members of the Church took other members in if they had any space or food left. Story after story showed the generosity of these humble people, taking no thought of their own comfort, just caring for the welfare of those in need. Those who possibly could do so made major contributions in money, in time, and in goods. There was an outpouring of love at all levels. Sympathy for the sufferer is apparently deeper and easier to demonstrate among the Latin Lamanite. They empathize with others, cry with others, and share everything they have unhesitantly.

I was impressed during a visit to El Salvador with the manner in which the Saints had worked together in a period of intense civil war fighting. During a terrorist offensive the streets were full of armed men from both sides. Running gun-fights in the neighborhoods were common. Heavier firepower was brought in from time to time by both sides to push the enemy out of the area, so this meant wholesale destruction of homes from bazookas, helicopter-borne rockets fired at the ground targets, and artillery pieces. Complete rows of homes were destroyed. I have pictures of parked cars looking like colanders from the hundreds of bullet holes in them. Families ran for cover in safer neighborhoods. Neighbors took in friends and strangers alike, sharing the beans, rice, tortillas, and anything else they had with them. Afterward, they would return together to the war-ravaged communities to gather in whatever they could salvage from the destruction. These are the true Samaritans.

At one particular time, a bishop and a stake president were attempting to deliver sacks of beans and rice to a few stranded families in the battle zone. They had covered only a few blocks when a running gunfire between the two sides came around a corner toward them. These two brethren hit the dirt, lying face down side by side, while bullets zipped overhead. The bishop wondered if they should not go home as soon as the fighting moved away from them, but the stake president said, "No, *hermano,* those families desperately need this food. The Lord will bless us while we are trying to help someone else." They waited a few moments longer and then were able to complete their errand of mercy.

Elder Dallin H. Oaks has said, "Whenever we focus on ourselves, even in our service to others, we fall short of the example of our Savior, who gave himself as a total and unqualified sacrifice for all mankind. Those who seek to follow his example must lose themselves in their service to others." (*Pure in Heart,* p. 46.) We have witnessed a grand army of good Samaritans, following Christ's example in losing themselves in their service to others—truly being the salt of the earth and a light unto the world.

CHAPTER 10

The Five Higher Laws
of the Gospel

After Christ taught the multitude the blessed beatitudes, he then admonished them, "Whosoever therefore shall break one of these least commandments, and shall teach men so, he shall be called the least in the kingdom of heaven: but whosoever shall do and teach them, the same shall be called great in the kingdom of heaven." (Matthew 5:19.)

The Savior then compared "big" sins, such as committing murder and adultery, to "insignificant" ones — the ones we are most likely to allow ourselves, such as becoming angry, lusting, judging, failing to forgive, savoring a little revenge, and nurturing the praise of men. He made it clear that these "unimportant" sins can make us turn away from his light and move toward the darkness of Satan without even being aware.

In each of the following, Christ compares the old law — the law of Moses — with the new: "Ye have heard that it hath been said by them of old time. . . . But I say unto you. . . . " What he is doing is pointing out a basic fallacy of conduct that all of Israel — the Jews and their Pharisees in particular — had fallen into. The Old Testament teaches that God desires internal purity, but the teachings of that day were mostly an external observance of the laws. The Savior brought a new and more complete way of coming unto him, and in order to

113

enter his kingdom and be with him eternally, a much higher and more strict observance would be required.

Anger

Book of Mormon: *"Ye have heard that it hath been said by them of old time . . . that thou shalt not kill. . . . But I say unto you, that whosoever is angry with his brother shall be in danger of [God's] judgment."* (3 Nephi 12:21–22.)

King James Version: *"Ye have heard that it was said by them of old time, Thou shalt not kill. . . . But I say unto you, That whosoever is angry with his brother without a cause shall be in danger of the judgment."* (Matthew 5:21–22.)

New Jerusalem Bible: *"You have learned how it was said to our ancestors: You must not kill. . . . But I say this to you: anyone who is angry with his brother will answer for it before the court."*

Phillips Modern English Bible: *"You have heard that it was said to the people in the old days, 'Thou shalt not murder.' . . . But I say to you that anyone who is angry with his brother must stand his trial."*

To the Jews, murder and any killing were prohibited; however, to Christ, a great deal of wickedness occurs long before that ultimate act, so he warns the people against any feelings or behavior that would lead up to it. Anger, hate, fury, hostility, extreme displeasure, exasperation, rage, violent feelings, and contention all fall into this category. Even feeling offended is a kind of anger that allows Satan to take over our thoughts and our actions, as much as if a poison had entered our system. Anger and its cousins are a poison and can lead to violence.

Many probably boasted that they had never killed, but with this new law they found themselves condemned for their hateful thoughts. God is a God of love, and uncontrolled negative passions are not part of his gospel; the person who has not learned to control them will not be welcomed in his presence — not in this life nor in the hereafter. The Holy Ghost is a peaceful influence and will also withdraw immediately from those who allow such emotions to take control of their minds, their hearts, their tongues, and their actions.

Any person still afflicted with such strong feelings has no claim on holiness or purity. Angry thoughts, expressions, and body language not only do damage to the individual, but when they exist they may also cause good people to shy away from that person's company. Even worse is that such rage or feelings of rage can also "murder" one's spirit. One's own personality and spirit is offended when he or she shows lack of maturity and control. Satan enjoys finding a person he can take over, and it is noticeable when he does. People who turn red in the face, shout, grimace, or gesture angrily are so ugly that they reflect the ugliness of Satan.

This scripture also includes the counsel that differences should be resolved quickly. Reconciliation is lauded — the sooner the better. In fact, the Lord says that we shouldn't even attempt to come unto him until we have resolved our differences with others. It is impossible for us to even worship him if anger is still in our hearts and minds. A visiting teaching message printed in the *Ensign* contains some everyday examples of times when anger is generated and some ideas on how to avoid it:

"One Sunday morning Betty got up late and had only forty-five minutes to get herself and her children ready for church. They would have been on time if it hadn't been for Susan's lost shoe and the jam on David's shirt. Betty felt angry with David and Susan, and she had difficulty feeling a spirit of reverence during the meetings.

"Nervous at the prospect of her first oral exam at the university, Dorothy waited in the hall for her professor for half an hour — which made her even more nervous. The first question he asked confused her, and her mind went blank. She stumbled through the rest of the exam, and he told her that she should reevaluate her ability to comprehend complex ideas. Dorothy felt frustrated and angry.

"At the supermarket, Helen watched the woman in front of her in line redeem forty-two dollars' worth of coupons. Everyone behind Helen moved to another line. When Helen joined them, she ended up behind five people, feeling angry and frustrated.

" 'Life is not fair,' said one woman after a hard day. 'The *whole world* provokes me!'

"Most of us feel frustrated or impatient at times. But when we express those feelings by becoming angry with someone, we offend the Spirit and invite bitterness into our hearts. As we strive to come unto Christ and to perfect ourselves, we should ask ourselves not 'What is fair?' but, humbly, 'What would Jesus have me do?' . . . Although most of us don't have to deal with persecution, we are often 'provoked' by small things. Rudeness, nagging, disobedience, waiting, disagreement, disappointments, and unfulfilled expectations can irritate us, particularly when we are tired, sick, or in a hurry. At such times, our first impulse may be to react with irritation, anger, or contention. But we can choose to react instead with charity and not be 'easily provoked.' . . .

"By learning to avoid contention and to control our anger, we stop evil from being passed along and become more like the Savior, whose sacrifice of self made eternal life possible for all who come unto him and emulate his example." ("Charity Is Not Easily Provoked," *Ensign,* July 1988, p. 47.)

Lust

Book of Mormon: *"It is written by them of old time, that thou shalt not commit adultery; but I say unto you, that whosoever looketh on a woman, to lust after her, hath committed adultery already in his heart."* (3 Nephi 12:27–30.)

King James Version: *"Ye have heard that it was said by them of* *old time, Thou shalt not commit adultery: but I say unto you, That whosoever looketh on a woman to lust after her hath committed adultery with her already in his heart."* (Matthew 5:27–30.)

Jerusalem Bible: *"You have learned how it was said: You must not commit adultery. But I say this to you: If a man looks at a woman lustfully, he has already committed adultery with her in his heart."*

Phillips Modern English Bible: *"You have heard that it was said to the people in the old days, 'Thou shalt not commit adultery.' But I say to you that every man who looks at a woman lustfully has already committed adultery with her — in his heart."*

Holy matrimony was declared and instituted by our Heavenly Father. In Genesis we read: "It is not good that the man should be alone. . . . Therefore shall a man leave his father and his mother, and shall cleave unto his wife: and they shall be one flesh." (Genesis 2:18, 24.) In the first chapter of Genesis God instructs males and females, whom he has created in his own image, to "be fruitful, and multiply." (Genesis 1:28.)

Through Joseph Smith, the Lord declared with resounding power that "marriage is ordained of God unto man." (D&C 49:15.) We also read in the Doctrine and Covenants that "in the celestial glory there are three heavens or degrees; and in order to obtain the highest, a man must enter into this order of the priesthood [meaning the new and everlasting covenant of marriage]; and if he does not, he cannot obtain it." (D&C 131:1–3.) In other words, not just any civil marriage is sufficient, but only the temple marriage and sealing will bring forth this promise.

Other scriptures given in this dispensation add information and guidance on the Old Testament theme of sexual purity. I am grateful to my dear friends, authors Blaine and Brenton Yorgason, for pointing out in their book *The Problem with Immorality* that there is a scripture that indicates three punishments for committing adultery in one's heart and another

117

that promises three rewards for virtuous thoughts. The three punishments for those who commit adultery in their heart are given in Doctrine and Covenants 63:16: (1) "they shall not have the Spirit"; (2) they "shall deny the faith"; and (3) they "shall fear" God's judgment.

The three rewards are listed in Doctrine and Covenants 121:45–46: (1) "then shall thy confidence wax strong in the presence of God"; (2) "the doctrine of the priesthood shall distil upon thy soul as the dews from heaven"; and 3) "the Holy Ghost shall be thy constant companion, and thy scepter an unchanging scepter of righteousness and truth."

The Lord has also warned against looking at anyone lustfully. In today's world that means literally what it says; in addition, it means not looking at pornographic magazines, movies, or television programs, or reading any books or material that is sexually explicit. There are books and articles of high tone and basic morality on the subject of sexual intimacy and no one need refer to base, ugly material for sex education.

No matter how much Satan tries to sell the idea that promiscuous sex is acceptable, the concept of a permanent marriage with a family life based upon loving and personal commitment is still the ideal. It is still the commandment of the Lord.

The Lord, in order to assure the continuance of the human race, has given us basic sexual instincts, but he has also given us limits on how to use them. His counsel on using these God-given sexual and procreative powers is to use them *only* within the bounds of marriage, with love and continual respect for each other's needs. A healthy dose of self-control is essential for every successful marriage. Paul seems to have been aware of the needs of both the man and the woman when he said, "To avoid fornication, let every man have his own wife, and let every woman have her own husband." (1 Corinthians 7:2.)

President Spencer W. Kimball wrote:

"I may not be able to eliminate pornographic trash, but my family and I need not buy or view it. . . . I may not be able to greatly reduce the divorces of the land or save all broken homes and frustrated children, but I can keep my own home a congenial one, my marriage happy, my home a heaven, and my children well adjusted. I may not be able to stop the growing claims to freedom from laws based on morals, or change all opinions regarding looseness in sex and growing perversions, but I can guarantee devotion to all high ideals and standards in my own home, and I can work toward giving my own family a happy, interdependent spiritual life." (*Faith Precedes the Miracle*, p. 247.)

In seeking for the way to "come unto Christ," we must search our own souls to discover if we are rising to higher levels of moral worthiness.

Oath-taking and Profanity

Book of Mormon: "*It is written, thou shalt not forswear thyself, but . . . I say unto you, swear not at all; . . . but let your communication be Yea, yea; Nay, nay.*" (3 Nephi 12:33–37.)

King James Version: "*It hath been said by them of old time, thou shalt not forswear thyself, . . . but I say unto you, Swear not at all; . . . let your communication be, Yea, yea; Nay, nay.*" (Matthew 5:33–37.)

New Jerusalem Bible: "*It was said to our ancestors: You must not break your oath, but must fulfill your oaths to the Lord. But I say this to you: do not swear at all. . . . All you need say is 'Yes' if you mean yes, 'No' if you mean no.*"

Phillips Modern English Bible: "*People in the old days were told—'Thou shalt not forswear thyself,' . . . but I say to you, don't use an oath at all. . . . Let your 'yes' be a plain 'yes' and your 'no' be a plain 'no.' *"

In the Old Testament, we learn that oath-taking was a normal and authorized procedure, somewhat like a legal contract today. The taking of oaths was apparently necessary because people did not live up to their word of honor. In fact, it appears that deceit, lying, falsehoods, and dishonesty were prevalent. Originally symbolic in nature, the taking of oaths became essential because of the lack of integrity in business matters, social relationships, and political matters. An individual's word could not be trusted, and in order to protect themselves, people came to assume that those with whom they did business were not completely honest and honorable in their dealings.

The dictionary defines the word *forswear* as to forsake, disavow, perjure, and swear falsely. This commandment is another way of saying, "Do not lie." It is possible that Christ was not only saying "Do not lie" but also, in effect, "Let your conduct be so pure, so above reproach, so honest and dependable that no one will think that they have to insist that you enter into a legal contract."

There was a time not too long ago when a person's word was his bond. My grandfather gave a verbal guarantee on a loan from a bank to a farmers' co-op whose project went sour. Since the bank had no legal recourse against the members, no one paid, so Grandfather Wells paid the whole debt at some sacrifice. Years later, another farmers' co-op from the same valley approached the same bank, but the employees in the bank were new, and no one remembered the old situation except one officer of the bank. He saw the name of Edwin Wells among the members of the co-op who were willing to guarantee the loan privately. He asked if Edwin was the son of Samuel Henry Wells, and was told that indeed he was. The banker responded, "We will make the loan. In fact, we would make the loan if that man were the only one giving his guarantee." All this came about because of the legacy of true honor and integrity that Grandfather Wells left.

Elder James E. Talmage told us that the Savior was saying

we have no right to take wanton oaths, reserving that for a solemn covenant or contract between God and man. He reminded us that the Savior said it is a sin to swear by heaven, which is the abode of God, or by earth, which is God's creation and his footstool. Then Elder Talmage wrote that "moderation in speech, decision and simplicity were enjoined [by the Savior], to the exclusion of expletives, profanity and oaths." (*Jesus the Christ*, 1983, p. 220.)

The advice that our language be limited to "Yea, yea" or "Nay, nay" is wise. Today, in many public places and in movies and TV programs, one can hear vulgar and filthy words that demonstrate a deficiency of vocabulary, a disintegration of culture, and a loss of simple decency. We all need to take the Lord's words at face value: "Swear not at all." What a much cleaner world we would have if the air were not polluted with vulgar expletives!

In addition to the sin of vulgarity, there is the sin of profanity, which is the misuse of sacred names and terms, words, and expressions. The taking of the name of Deity, either the Father or the Son, in vain is blasphemy and removes the perpetrator far from the influence of divinity, which does not tolerate that offense. Included in this vile practice is the use of a shortened version of our Savior's name, Jesus, which has been shortened to the irreverent slang expression "Jeez and "gee." Just as vile is the shortened version of "Golly"— reduced to "Gol"—which is close to the title given to our Father in heaven and to his Son, Jesus Christ. How offensive this must be to those holy beings we worship! To come unto the Savior involves removing these habits from our tongues, mouths, thoughts, and minds.

President Gordon B. Hinckley gave a timely sermon on the subject of profanity in a general conference address in October 1987. He stated, "The habit . . . which some young people fall into, of using vulgarity and profanity . . . is not only offensive . . . but it is a gross sin in the sight of God and should not exist among the children of the Latter-day Saints." (*Ensign*, November 1987, p. 46.) President Hinckley's entire sermon deserves to be read and reread.

The *Church News* some time ago published the following suggestions from readers on "How to Rid Children's Speech of Profanity":

"When I returned from my mission, I brought my 15-year-old granddaughter home to live with me for a year or two. I soon realized that her speech was certainly not acceptable in polite society. However, I didn't know how to go about helping her stop. I prayed for a quick miracle. After much anguish and concern, the following solution came to my mind: I gave her a $50 bill and explained to her that it was a gift with a 'string' attached. The bill was hers to keep or spend, but for every unacceptable word she uttered, she had to forfeit $1. It really worked a miracle. Never once again did I hear a single vulgar word from her. I did get a chuckle, however, when she called me from school and all she said was, 'Grandma, I owe you $2.' The $50 was a small price to pay for an instant miracle." (Winifred Smith.)

"Nothing is more effective in halting the habit of using foul language than eliminating the use of any word that even resembles an expletive. This goes for such mild words as heck, darn, gee whiz, etc., and many others meant to be humorous. Replace these words with others describing how you feel. It would benefit all if everyone would learn to say precisely what they mean and no more. Properly explaining what is intended to be communicated becomes a talent much admired and should be constantly cultivated." (M.B. Hipwell.)

The suggestions concluded with a checklist:

"1. Teach your children to think before they speak.

"2. Set the example for children by using proper language.

"3. Explain what the words mean and why they're demeaning.

"4. Pray for ways to help youth clean up their speech." (*Church News*, December 26, 1987, p. 15.)

As we become examples of true believers, especially in word and deed, we can be instruments for the Lord in helping to lift others to a higher level. This is illustrated in the following experience:

A group of young people, with their advisor, were traveling on a chartered bus from the Midwest to attend the Hill Cumorah Pageant in New York. About midway along the journey the bus broke down, and the driver had to get out and try to fix it. As he lay under the big vehicle in the blistering heat, he was heard to utter expletives, including using the name of the Lord in vain. Soon the teenagers got off the bus, formed a circle around the man, and began singing "I Am a Child of God." The driver listened, stopped what he was doing, stood up, and, with tears in his eyes, apologized for his uncouth language. He was so impressed with these young people that when they arrived at their destination, he asked to learn more about "that religion that teaches people how to live better lives." This teachable man and his family were baptized.

Whether it be the issue of honor as opposed to lying, or clean language as opposed to vulgarity and profanity, it is clear that the way to draw closer to the Savior is to understand the power of the tongue and the things we say. Let us use this God-given power to praise and worship him, not to offend him and cause his Spirit to withdraw from us. This truly is a higher law — in every sense.

An Eye for An Eye

Book of Mormon: "*It is written, an eye for an eye, and a tooth for a tooth; but I say unto you, that ye shall not resist evil, but whosoever shall smite thee on thy right cheek, turn to him the other* *also; and if any man will sue thee at the law and take away thy coat, let him have thy cloak also; and whosoever shall compel thee to go a mile, go with him twain."* (3 Nephi 12:38–42.)

King James Version: *"It hath been said, An eye for an eye, and a tooth for a tooth: but I say unto you, That ye resist not evil: But whosoever shall smite thee on thy right cheek, turn to him the other also. And if any man will sue thee at the law, and take away thy coat, let him have thy cloke also. And whosoever shall compel thee to go a mile, go with him twain."* (Matthew 5:38–42.)

New Jerusalem Bible: *"It was said: Eye for eye and tooth for tooth. But I say this to you: offer the wicked man no resistance. On the contrary, if anyone hits you on the right cheek, offer him the other as well; if a man takes you to law and would have your tunic, let him have your cloak as well. And if anyone orders you to go one mile, go two miles with him."*

Phillips Modern English Bible: *"It used to be said 'An eye for an eye and a tooth for a tooth', but I tell you, don't resist evil. If a man hits your right cheek, turn the other one to him as well. If a man wants to sue you for your coat, let him have it and your cloak as well. If anybody forces you to go a mile with him, do more—go two miles with him."*

The law or principle of retribution is of ancient origin and was well-known to the Jews at the time of Jesus. The fact that the Master gave a new and higher law was not easily understood after so many generations of what the Jews thought was strict justice and fair compensation. Jesus himself was the supreme example of this principle when he stood submissively before the Jewish and Roman courts. Underlining his demeanor was the magnificence of pure Christian love. When you truly love another person, or the group that individual may represent, or the society of which he is a part, then you do not react to any one person's abuse but rather submit in peaceful dignity, as did the Savior to his persecutors. The way of the Lord is one of patience, understanding, and forgiveness.

Paul understood this principle, as did Mormon. Both received their inspiration from the Savior's example and from their Heavenly Father through the Holy Ghost. Each gave a major sermon on the importance of love; Paul, in 1 Corinthians 13, and Mormon, in the Book of Mormon, Moroni 7, say almost the same thing. Both sermons are so similar that they might have come from the same script. In fact, each of these prophets was guided by the same Holy Spirit from on high.

Paul and Mormon both define the way we should act if we are full of the pure love of Christ. Call it mercy, call it charity, call it the love of Christ: it still motivates us to react in the same way in the face of opposition, misunderstanding, abuse, and frustration. Paul says to bear all things and to endure all things. That is the pathway to Christ.

The Savior's statement "And whosoever shall compel thee to go a mile, go with him twain" sometimes requires of the disciple of Christ great sacrifice, but by following his command, we are given opportunities to serve others.

The following story, quoted by Elder Vaughn J. Featherstone, points to this important counsel of the Master:

"In ancient . . . times, soldiers could force teenage boys in Roman provinces to carry their heavy backpacks for one mile, but no more. In a typical scene, we would see a soldier walk into a community. . . . The soldier [sees] the boy and motions for him to come and pick up the heavy backpack. Reluctantly, the boy shoulders the heavy load. The soldier motions toward the road leading out of town, and together they trudge toward the first mile marker.

"When the marker comes into sight, the soldier motions for the boy to put the pack down. The boy instead agrees to carry the pack another mile. The soldier reminds him that only one mile is required. However, the boy agrees to go 'the second mile.' As they continue down the road, the soldier begins to talk with the boy. He asks him if he has seen the mighty ocean. The boy replies 'no,' so the soldier gives descriptive accounts of his adventures on the high seas. The soldier then relates stories about military campaigns in distant countries and describes snow covered mountains, which the lad has never seen.

"The vivid accounts stir the imagination of the young lad as he hears the tales of the seas and of distant lands. The second mile goes quickly, and the boy discovers the secret of 'going the second mile.' You go the first mile and you discharge a duty; you go the second mile and you make a friend. The great men and women in history have been those willing to go the second mile. (Beverly Chiodo, 'Vital Speeches of the Day,' November 1987, p. 42.)"

We all have assignments and things we must do. The temptation is to just get them over with. Yet real joy and satisfaction — and greatness — come from going beyond the mere requirements. Elder Featherstone goes on to say: "History shows that there have been a number of people who have learned this great secret, that when service is freely given it becomes sweet. In going the second mile, these people honor our Heavenly Father by honoring themselves and honoring others. Those who go the second mile are often blessed with another rare and unique gift — they discover the divine in others. When we consider that every soul who walks the earth may become like our spiritual Father in heaven, it should humble us in the presence of any human soul." ("The Message: Secret of the Second Mile," *New Era*, May 1990, pp. 4–6.)

Hate Thine Enemy

Book of Mormon: *"It is written also, that thou shalt love thy neighbor and hate thine enemy; but behold I say unto you, love your enemies, bless them that curse you, do good to them that hate you, and pray for them who despitefully use you and persecute you."* (3 Nephi 12:43–46.)

King James Version: *"It hath been said, Thou shalt love thy neighbour, and hate thine enemy. But I say unto you, Love your enemies, bless them that curse you, do good to them that hate you,*

and pray for them which despitefully use you, and persecute you."
(Matthew 5:43–46.)

New Jerusalem Bible: "*It was said: You must love your neighbor and hate your enemy. But I say this to you: love your enemies and pray for those who persecute you.*"

Phillips Modern English Bible: "*It used to be said 'Thou shalt love thy neighbour and hate thine enemy', but I tell you, 'Love your enemies, and pray for those who persecute you.'*"

As we consider the issue of the higher laws, we might ask ourselves, Just how good do I have to be to please the Lord? If we hunger and thirst after righteousness we will ask the question not to find out if we are good enough, but in order to keep seeking constantly to lift ourselves to a higher level. The scriptures in this section of the Sermon on the Mount give us a very strict standard to follow, but we must follow it if we are going to progress in coming to Christ.

The following is a story of a sister who turned hate to forgiveness and learned of the love of Christ:

"Christl Fechter, a Czechoslovakian refugee, faced this challenge [of overcoming hate] and, with the Lord's help, overcame it. As a young woman, she was forced by political upheaval to leave her homeland for Germany. There she learned about the Church and was baptized in 1958. A year later, she moved to the United States, settling in Bountiful, Utah. While living in Utah, she was terribly hurt emotionally by someone and, for the first time in her life, felt hatred.

" 'I had been through all the terrors of the invasion of my country, but I had never before experienced the feeling of hate,' she says. 'It changed my personality. Even my non-member friends realized that I was not the same person any more.' . . .

"One day she read [the scripture about 'loving your enemies.'] . . . Christl felt that this passage was meant just for her. 'I could not imagine myself praying for this person, but

I wanted to do what the Lord said, and I knew I had to get rid of the hatred,' she says. So she knelt that night and prayed, with reservations, that the Lord would bless the person who had hurt her.

"She felt a little better. The next night she prayed again, this time wholeheartedly, and she immediately felt the hatred lift from her, never to return. She discovered that the Lord could pour out his Spirit upon her and teach her to love as he does." ("Charity Seeketh Not Her Own," *Ensign,* June 1988, p. 53.)

Our daughter Elayne served in the Ecuador Guayaquil Mission. In one of her letters, she shared the following beautiful experience concerning loving those who have been responsible for hurt and emotional pain: "What a change has come over (Blanca) since we've been teaching her. In our second discussion, when we talked of repentance, I felt impressed to say that we need to forgive others in order to be forgiven. She said she could not forgive, that she had been hurt badly by many people, and that it would be impossible to forgive them. One could tell just in meeting her for the first time that she had been through a lot of pain and emotional trauma; her eyes were full of hurt, like a wounded puppy, and she would barely kiss us hello. . . . I read her some scriptures on forgiveness, and explained to her how prayer would give her strength to forgive. What a change since then! Light shines in her eyes, and she hugs us every time we come to visit, she's doing a lot of reading in the Book of Mormon, and most important, she told us that she has completely forgiven all the people who had hurt her, and feels completely content and full of peace."

In his Sermon on the Mount, this significant new doctrine was one of Jesus' most electrifying teachings. Never before had the people of Israel been required to love their enemies! In the scripture "an eye for an eye, and a tooth for a tooth," he *changed* the old rule of retribution, but now he *added* something: he told his listeners, "Love your enemies, bless them that curse you, do good to them that hate you, and pray for them which despitefully use you, and persecute you." The Master knew that this was one of the hardest of the new higher commandments; therefore, he added a promise to those who live it: "that ye may be the children of your Father which is in heaven." Then he asked a question, perhaps to cause reflection: "For if ye love them which love you, what reward have ye? do not even the publicans the same?" (Matthew 5:46.)

Charlotte Bronte wrote: "Life appears to me to be too short to be spent in nursing animosity or in registering wrongs. We are, and must be, one and all, burdened with faults in this world; but the time will come when, I trust, we shall put them off in putting off our corruptible bodies; when debasement and sin will fall from us and only the spark will remain. . . . With this creed, revenge never worries my heart, degradation never too deeply disgusts me, injustice never crushes me too low." (Quoted in Lillian Eichler Watson, ed., *Light from Many Lamps*, pp. 201–2.)

Someone once said that people are spiritual beings. Something within them urges them to rise above themselves — to control themselves and their environment — to master the body, the mind, and the tongue, and to live in a more perfect and peaceful world. We are of divine origin — children of a supreme God. We must seek out those higher, celestial levels.

·

CHAPTER 11

The Highest Law of All:
Be Ye Perfect

Book of Mormon: *"Therefore I would that ye should be perfect even as I, or your Father who is in heaven is perfect."* (3 Nephi 12:48.)

King James Version: *"Be ye therefore perfect, even as your Father which is in heaven is perfect."* (Matthew 5:48.)

New Jerusalem Bible: *"You must therefore be perfect just as your heavenly Father is perfect."*

Phillips Modern English Bible: *"You will be perfect as your Heavenly Father is perfect."*

The Savior could have placed this commandment at the very beginning of the Sermon on the Mount, or he could have placed it at the very end of his sermon as a summary of what he has given to all mankind. Instead, he chose to place it immediately after the five higher laws of Christian conduct. He leads into it with a reminder that if we who try to follow him are only like other people, we do not have much claim on special blessings. He says, "If ye love them which love you, what reward have ye? . . . And if ye salute your brethren only, what do ye more than others? do not even the publicans [do the same]?" (Matthew 5:46–47.) The publicans were especially despised by the Jews because they collected duties and taxes and were noticeably corrupt in taking bribes. Yet they loved their own and greeted their own. It is a strong lesson the Master is teaching here.

"Of him unto whom much is given much is required." (D&C 82:3.) Christ expects a great deal from those who follow him. It is not a path for the fainthearted or the weak, for there are many trials and tests to overcome along the way. The reward is great, but the Savior is giving a new and higher law than ever before imagined. Now the crowning jewel on that string of thoughts is the injunction to be perfect. In the New Testament version he says we should be perfect "even as your Father which is in heaven." In the Book of Mormon account, he says we should be perfect "even as I, or your Father who is in heaven is perfect." We do not know if he includes himself as being perfect in the Book of Mormon record because he is a resurrected God when he speaks to those in the Americas or if the original statement from New Testament times has been lost. Unequivocally, we accept Christ as perfect both during his mortal life and after his resurrection.

In the closing pages of the Book of Mormon is Moroni's poignant and stirring farewell to the Lamanites, urging them, and all of us, to "come unto Christ, and be perfected in him." We are admonished, "Deny yourselves of all ungodliness; and if ye shall deny yourselves of all ungodliness, and love God with all your might, mind and strength, then is his grace sufficient for you, that by his grace ye may be perfect in Christ; and if by the grace of God ye are perfect in Christ, ye can in nowise deny the power of God." (Moroni 10:32.) Jesus showed clearly that perfection is a gift to those who have partaken of the grace of God through their righteousness and obedience. By itself, our righteousness could never make us perfect as our Father in heaven is perfect. But through the atonement of Christ and the influence of the Holy Ghost, we can become sanctified and made perfect.

However, all this is conditional: we must first have faith

in him, repent, be baptized by immersion for the remission of sins, and receive the Holy Ghost, that we may be guided constantly. Then, if we remain faithful until the end, his grace will pay the price for our imperfections. We will fall short of the perfection we seek in this life because we are mortal and are subject, because of the flesh, to myriad tests and struggles with sin and also to the influence of Satan. But we are promised that the Lord can give us his divine nature *if* we follow him. Peter tells us, "According as his divine power hath given unto us all things that pertain unto life and godliness, through the knowledge of him that hath called us to glory and virtue: whereby are given unto us exceeding great and precious promises: that by these [we] might be partakers of the divine nature." (2 Peter 1:3–4.)

The original Greek word for perfect is *teleios*, which means whole or finished. When we have sincere hunger and thirst for righteousness and a burning desire to become more like the pure example of our Savior, then we make daily progress toward perfection until we become a "finished product." Although it is a sort of do-it-yourself project, the Lord will help us as we help ourselves. A good brother in a testimony meeting in Mexico recently stated, "The Lord is really helping me perfect myself. He magnifies my efforts. When I try to do something good he multiplies my efforts in a great way, but when I do nothing, the Lord with mathematical precision does exactly nothing also." As we try to become more perfect, our Father in heaven will help make us complete or whole.

Elder James E. Talmage gives a clear explanation of this concept of perfection. He says: "Our Lord's admonition to men to become perfect, even as the Father is perfect (Matt. 5:48) cannot rationally be construed otherwise than as implying the possibility of such achievement. Plainly, however, man cannot become perfect in mortality in the sense in which God is perfect as a supremely glorified Being. It is possible, though, for man to be perfect in his sphere in a sense analogous to that in which superior intelligences are perfect in their several spheres; yet the relative perfection of the lower is infinitely inferior to that of the higher. A college student in his freshman or sophomore year may be perfect as freshman or sophomore; his record may possibly be a hundred percent on the scale of efficiency and achievement; yet the honors of the upper classman are beyond him, and the attainment of graduation is to him remote, but of assured possibility, if he [does] but continue faithful and devoted to the end." (*Jesus the Christ*, 1983, p. 232.)

The commandment that we be perfect may seem difficult, but through the purifying influence of the Holy Ghost, it is a goal that is not only attainable, but necessary to our salvation. Elder Bruce R. McConkie has given comfort and encouragement to those who try to become perfect in an imperfect world: "We have to become perfect to be saved in the celestial kingdom. But nobody becomes perfect in this life. Only the Lord Jesus attained that state, and he had an advantage that none of us has. He was the Son of God. . . . He lived a perfect life, and he set an ideal example. . . . As it is with being born again, and as it is with sanctifying our souls, so becoming perfect in Christ is a process.

"We begin to keep the commandments today, and we keep more of them tomorrow, and we go from grace to grace, up the steps of the ladder, and we thus improve and perfect our souls. We can become perfect in some minor things. We can be perfect in the payment of tithing. If we pay one-tenth of our interest annually into the tithing funds of the Church, if we do it year in and year out, and desire to do it, and have no intent to withhold, and if we would do it regardless of what arose in our lives, then in that thing we are perfect. . . .

"As members of the Church, if we chart a course leading to eternal life; if we begin the processes of spiritual rebirth, and are going in the right direction; if we chart a course of sanctifying our souls, and degree by degree are going in that direction; and if we chart a course of becoming perfect, and, step by step and phase by phase, are perfecting our souls by overcoming the world, then it is absolutely guaranteed—there is no question whatever about it—we shall gain eternal life. Even though we have spiritual rebirth ahead of us, perfection ahead of us, the full degree of sanctification ahead of us, if we chart a course and follow it to the best of our ability in this life, then when we go out of this life we'll continue in exactly that same course. . . .

"The Prophet [Joseph Smith] told us that there are many things that people have to do, even after the grave, to work out their salvation. We're not going to be perfect the minute we die. But if we've charted a course, if our desires are right, if our appetites are curtailed and bridled, and if we believe in the Lord and are doing to the very best of our abilities what we ought to do, we'll go on to everlasting salvation, which is the fulness of eternal reward in our Father's kingdom." (*BYU Speeches of the Year,* 1976, pp. 399–401.)

As Elder McConkie pointed out, we can be absolutely perfect in some things. We can and must be perfect in maintaining our virtue. It is possible to be chaste before marriage. It may be more difficult to follow the higher law of controlling our thoughts, but we can stay far away enough from danger and temptation that loss of chastity never happens. We can be perfect in abstinence from prohibited substances. We can be perfect in our home teaching and other church callings. We can be perfect in many other areas of our life, thus bringing comfort and peace into our lives while we are on this earth.

As we become renewed by the Spirit through striving for perfection and coming unto Christ, we will eventually see the promises fulfilled of enjoying immortal glory and exaltation with our Father in heaven and our Savior.

Three Rules Against Hypocrisy

The next three subjects in the Sermon on the Mount deal with the importance of performing sacred acts with sincerity of purpose rather than as hypocrites, with selfish, hidden motives, to be seen of men. Those who profess to be righteous but who do things to be seen of men will have their earthly reward from men. They will not be seen of God nor rewarded of God. The Savior would have his disciples follow his commandments motivated by sincere love and not for the server's riches, own recognition, or the honors and praises of others. Any time the giver acts with a hidden, selfish motive, performed under the guise of goodness, he or she does not have a pure heart.

The Savior was more concerned with internal feelings and intents of the heart than with external manifestations. He declared, "Woe unto you, . . . for ye are like unto whited sepulchres, which indeed appear beautiful outward, but are within full of dead men's bones, and of all uncleanness. Even so ye also outwardly appear righteous unto men, but within ye are full of hypocrisy and iniquity." (Matthew 23:27–28.) In the Sermon on the Mount, the Lord gives only three illustrations that refer to common daily experiences, but we find many examples throughout the scriptures in which he denounced hypocrisy.

President David O. McKay stated: "Mere compliance with

the word of the Lord, without a corresponding inward desire, will avail but little. Indeed, such outward actions and pretending phrases may disclose hypocrisy, a sin that Jesus most vehemently condemned." (Conference Report, October 1951, p. 6.)

Most of us, at some time or other, are guilty to some extent of desiring to be seen or recognized, and we need to control this self-serving attitude. Our good works and acts must be for the glorifying of our Father in heaven and his Son, Jesus Christ, or we will lose our own reward and be found guilty of hypocrisy, a sin exemplified by the Pharisees and scribes of old. Hypocrisy is related to pride and ego; all are stumbling blocks along our path to coming unto Christ.

Do Not Your Alms to Be Seen of Men

Book of Mormon: *"I would that ye should do alms unto the poor; but take heed that ye do not your alms before men to be seen of them; otherwise ye have no reward of your Father who is in heaven. Therefore, when ye shall do your alms do not sound a trumpet before you, as will hypocrites do in the synagogues and in the streets, that they may have glory of men. Verily I say unto you, they have their reward. But when thou doest alms let not thy left hand know what thy right hand doeth; that thine alms may be in secret; and thy Father who seeth in secret, himself shall reward thee openly."* (3 Nephi 13:1–4.)

King James Version: *"Do not your alms before men, to be seen of them: otherwise ye have no reward of your Father which is in heaven. Therefore when thou doest thine alms, do not sound a trumpet before thee, as the hypocrites do in the synagogues and in the streets, that they may have glory of men. . . . They have their reward. But when thou doest alms, let not thy left hand know what thy right hand doeth: that thine alms may be in secret: and thy Father which seeth in secret himself shall reward thee openly."* (Matthew 6:1–4.)

Jerusalem Bible: *"Be careful not to parade your good deeds before men to attract their notice; by doing this you will lose all reward from your Father in heaven. So when you give alms, do not have* *it trumpeted before you; this is what the hypocrites do in the synagogues and in the streets to win men's admiration. I tell you solemnly, they have had their reward."*

Phillips Modern English Bible: *"Beware of doing your good deeds conspicuously to catch men's eyes or you will miss the reward of your Heavenly Father. So, when you do good to other people, don't hire a trumpeter to go in front of you—like those play-actors in the synagogues and streets who make sure that men admire them. Believe me, they have had all the reward they are going to get!"*

This statement deals not only with giving donations to the Church, to any good cause, or directly to a needy person, but also with serving, as shown in both the Jerusalem and Phillips translations. The Book of Mormon account begins with a meaningful statement that is missing in the other three translations. Undoubtedly the Savior included this concept originally but it has been lost. The scripture in 3 Nephi says that the Lord wants us to give to the poor. The other three versions omit this phrase, giving an impression that the Lord may not be as interested in the doing as in the "how" of being generous. King Benjamin, in the Book of Mormon, declared in his temple sermon that in order to *retain* a remission of our sins (he uses the word *retain*, since we *obtained* remission when we were baptized), we must impart of our substance to the poor. (See Mosiah 4:26.)

I feel that the Phillips translation is the most clear of all the translations. We have heard that we should not "blow our own horn," but here the translator says that the Savior warned, "Don't hire a trumpeter to go in front of you like those play-actors in the synagogues." We know that ostentation and hypocritical display are misplaced motives for donating. In Christ's church, seldom do we find plaques honoring those who donated the organ or the pews or a piece of artwork, as is common in other churches. Frequently an organization will honor a major donor by naming a room or wing of a building, or sometimes an entire edifice, after him or her. If that is a condition of the gift, then the motive of giving is improperly placed; but if the gift is made unconditionally and the authorities afterwards decide to honor the donor by naming something after him or her, that act would be acceptable under Christ's law of giving.

We have heard of some businessmen who make donations in hopes of getting publicity that will lead to an increase in sales and allow them to recoup more than the donation in increased profits. We have heard of some who hope their generosity will result in free press coverage or an advantage with influential parties. The Savior said clearly that they have their reward from exactly that which they sought, but that they cannot expect any reward from our Heavenly Father. Unless motivated by pure, unselfish reasons, even the most generous gifts profit nothing. The Savior taught that almsgiving should be made in secret, and then the reward shall be given according to the will of the Lord, in secret or openly, in this life or in the eternities.

In his April 1990 general conference address, Elder Marvin J. Ashton spoke of the sin of boasting of mighty works. He quoted from the Sermon on the Mount, "let not thy left hand know what thy right hand doeth," and then said, "Whatever success we might have had as we have tried to help should usually not be discussed, let alone boasted about. Humble, quiet, compassionate service is so soul-rewarding; who would need to point out the subject or location of kindly deeds? 'For although a man may have many revelations, and have power to do many mighty works, yet if he boasts in his own strength, and sets at naught the counsels of God, and follows after the dictates of his own will and carnal desires, he must fall and incur the vengeance of a just God upon him.' (D&C 3:4.)" (*Ensign*, May 1990, p. 66.)

Elder J. Richard Clarke, then second counselor in the

Presiding Bishopric, said in his October 1981 general conference address, "We demonstrate the depth of our love for the Savior when we care enough to seek out the suffering among us and attend to their needs. . . . We would all like to have the Savior's capacity to assuage the hungers of the world; but let us not forget that there are many simple ways by which we can walk in His steps. Let us remember that in giving of ourselves, it is less a question of giving a lot than of giving at the right moment." (Conference Report, October 1981, pp. 112–13.)

Two of our daughters had the privilege of visiting Israel and walking where Jesus walked. They learned in greater depth what it means to follow the Master. How *do* we follow the Master? "When we serve others — lift the weak, feed the hungry, comfort the bereaved, tend the sick, visit the prisoner — we are, in essence, following the Savior. In our own way, we are walking as he walked." ("In His Footsteps," *Church News*, February 10, 1990, p. 16.)

This message is beautifully expressed in a hymn we sing often in church:

> Have I done any good in the world today?
> Have I helped anyone in need?
> Have I cheered up the sad and made someone feel glad?
> If not, I have failed indeed.
>
> Has anyone's burden been lighter today
> Because I was willing to share?
> Have the sick and the weary been helped on their way?
> When they needed my help was I there?
>
> Then wake up and do something more
> Than dream of your mansion above.
> Doing good is a pleasure, a joy beyond measure,
> A blessing of duty and love.
> —*Hymns*, no. 223

Pray Not as the Hypocrites

Book of Mormon: *"When thou prayest thou shalt not do as the hypocrites, for they love to pray, standing in the synagogues and in the corners of the streets, that they may be seen of men. Verily I say unto you, they have their reward. But thou, when thou prayest, enter into thy closet, and when thou hast shut thy door, pray to thy Father who is in secret; and thy Father, who seeth in secret, shall reward thee openly. But when ye pray, use not vain repetitions, as the heathen, for they think that they shall be heard for their much speaking. Be not ye therefore like unto them, for your Father knoweth what things ye have need of before ye ask him. After this manner therefore pray ye: Our Father who art in heaven, hallowed be thy name. Thy will be done on earth as it is in heaven. And forgive us our debts, as we forgive our debtors. And lead us not into temptation, but deliver us from evil. For thine is the kingdom, and the power, and the glory, forever. Amen."* (3 Nephi 13:5–13.)

King James Version: This translation of Matthew 6:5–13 is close enough to the version in the Book of Mormon that it does not need to be repeated.

Jerusalem Bible: *"When you pray, do not imitate the hypocrites: they love to say their prayers standing up in the synagogues and at the street corners for people to see them. I tell you solemnly, they have had their reward. But when you pray, go to your private room and, when you have shut your door, pray to your Father who is in that secret place, and your Father who sees all that is done in secret, will reward you. In your prayers do not babble as the pagans do, for they think that by using many words they will make themselves heard. Do not be like them; your Father knows what you need before you ask him. So you should pray like this: Our father in heaven, may your name be held holy, your kingdom come, your will be done, on earth as in heaven. Give us today our daily bread. And forgive us our debts, as we have forgiven those who are in debt to us. And do not put us to the test, but save us from the evil one."*

Phillips Modern English Bible: This version of Matthew 6:5–13 is enough like the Jerusalem Bible version that it need not be repeated.

Frequent, daily prayer is a basic requirement of the faithful disciple of Christ. If we make a habit of sincere prayer, our lives will be noticeably and profoundly altered. Those prayers that come from the heart, recognizing our dependence upon our Heavenly Father, can change our actions and demeanor and bring us closer to Christ.

The Joseph Smith Translation of the Bible provides one significant new insight on the Lord's Prayer. Both the Book of Mormon and the King James Version read, "Lead us not into temptation." The Joseph Smith Translation is more explicit. It does not seem right that the Lord would "lead" us into temptation—Satan has that distinction. The Joseph Smith Translation reads: "*Suffer us not to be led* into temptation." In the Phillips Modern Bible, the line reads "*Keep us clear* of temptation."

The Lord's Prayer is very short, perhaps only twenty seconds in length. Following the example given by Jesus, we should keep our prayers simple, direct, and sincere. When we pray in public, we should pray in the plural voice ("we," not "I"), and we have been counseled to use the respectful forms of "thee" and "thou" instead of the familiar form of "you." It is not appropriate to preach a sermon in a prayer. Also, public prayers to open and close meetings should be relatively short. For example, those who offer prayers in general conference sessions are instructed to limit their invocation or benediction to no more than two minutes; and sometimes when the person who is to give the prayer reaches the pulpit, a note indicates that time is short and a shorter prayer would be appreciated. We need to be flexible and sensitive to the desires of those who preside. Prayers in the Church of Jesus Christ are offered through the Spirit, with no memorized nor written script, although we can have in mind pertinent subjects that concern everyone and that we wish to remember in the prayer, such as recent events to be grateful for, special needs of the congregation (such as for rain during a time of drought), and the names of persons who are ill.

In our prayers, both private and public, the important thing to remember is that repetition and words without "real intent of heart," as Mormon preached, will bring no blessings, and God will not receive them. We should avoid exaggerated styles of speaking. Our words should be sweet and without affectation, artistry, distortions, or anything else that might call attention to us and detract from what we are saying. It is not necessary to use an impressive vocabulary, since the Lord does not need to be impressed, and it is wrong to try to impress anyone else. As the Savior said, if those who are praying want to impress anyone here on earth, they will have had their reward, but the reward of the Lord will not come to them.

When we speak of coming unto Christ, we do not mean that we should pray to Christ directly. He has commanded us to pray to the Father in his name. Elder Bruce R. McConkie clearly explained that some misguided members may "begin to pray directly to Christ because of some special friendship they feel has been developed [with him]. . . . This is . . . non-sense. Our prayers are addressed to the Father, and to him only. . . . [They are] answered in whatever way seems proper by him who [knows] the needs of his children." (*BYU Speeches of the Year,* 1981–82, p. 102.)

President Ezra Taft Benson has given us five ways to improve our communication with our Heavenly Father:

"1. *We should pray frequently.* We should be alone with our Heavenly Father at least two or three times each day. . . . In addition, we are told to pray always. This means that our hearts should be full, drawn out in prayer unto our Heavenly Father continually.

"2. *We should find an appropriate place where we can meditate and pray.* We are admonished that this should be 'in [our] closets, and [our] secret places, and in [our] wilderness.' (Alma

34:26.) That is, it should be free from distraction, in se-cret. . . .

"3. *We should prepare ourselves for prayer.* If we do not feel like praying, then we should pray until we do feel like praying. We should be humble. We should pray for forgiveness and mercy. We must forgive anyone against whom we have bad feelings. . . .

"4. *Our prayers should be meaningful and pertinent.* We should avoid using the same phrases in each prayer. Any of us would become offended if a friend said the same words to us each day, treated the conversation as a chore, and could hardly wait to finish in order to turn on the television and forget us. . . . We should pray about our work, against the power of our enemies and devil, for our welfare and the welfare of those around us. We should counsel with the Lord regarding all our decisions and activities. . . . We should be grateful enough to give thanks for all we have. . . .

"5. *After making a request through prayer, we have a re-sponsibility to assist in its being granted.* We should listen. Perhaps while we are on our knees, the Lord wants to counsel us." ("Pray Always," *Ensign,* February 1990, pp. 2–4.)

Alexis Carrel, a physician, wrote: "Prayer is not only wor-ship; it is also an invisible emanation of man's worshiping spirit — the most powerful form of energy that one can gen-erate. . . . Only in prayer do we achieve that complete and harmonious assembly of body, mind, and spirit which gives the frail human reed its unshakable strength." (Lillian Eichler Watson, ed., *Light from Many Lamps,* pp. 66–67.)

It is significant to note that after giving his model prayer, the Master elaborated on the principle of forgiveness, as men-tioned in the prayer, saying: "If ye forgive men their trespasses, your heavenly Father will also forgive you: but if ye forgive not men their trespasses, neither will your Father forgive your trespasses." (Matthew 6:14–15.) He later taught this principle through a parable about a king who had two servants. One of the servants owed a large sum of money to the king, but the king forgave him the debt. The second servant owed the first a small sum; however, the first servant would not forgive that debt. When the king learned of this, he severely chastised the first servant, saying, "O thou wicked servant, I forgave thee all that debt. . . . Shouldest not thou also have had compassion on thy fellowservant, even as I had pity on thee?" And the king "delivered him to the tormentors." (Matthew 18:23–35.)

When Ye Fast Be Not as the Hypocrites

Book of Mormon: *"When ye fast be not as the hypocrites, of a sad countenance, for they disfigure their faces that they may appear unto men to fast. . . . They have their reward. But thou, when thou fastest, . . . appear not unto men to fast, but unto thy Father who is in secret; and thy Father, who seeth in secret, shall reward thee openly."* (3 Nephi 13:16–18.)

King James Version: *"When ye fast, be not, as the hypocrites, of a sad countenance: for they disfigure their faces, that they may appear unto men to fast. . . . They have their reward. But thou, when thou fastest, . . . appear not unto men to fast, but unto thy Father which is in secret: and thy Father, which seeth in secret, shall reward thee openly."* (Matthew 6:16–18.)

Jerusalem Bible: *"When you fast do not put on a gloomy look as the hypocrites do: they pull long faces to let men know they are fasting. . . . They have had their reward. . . . But when you fast . . . [let] no one know you are fasting except your Father who sees all that is done in secret: and your Father who sees all that is done in secret will reward you."*

Phillips Modern English Bible: *"When you fast, don't look like those miserable play-actors! For they deliberately disfigure their faces so that people may see that they are fasting. Believe me, they have had all their reward. No, when you fast, . . . [do it] so that nobody knows that you are fasting—let it be a secret between you and your Father. And your Father who knows all secrets will reward you."*

144

Special blessings come from fasting when our fast is motivated by our love of the Savior. Fasting is a major part of the process of drawing us closer to Jesus Christ and our Father in heaven. The Church provides an inspired, organized way of responding to the needs of others. Members are asked to set aside a little from their abundance and donate it to the fast offering fund. Since no one knows how much the donation is, this remains anonymous — an example of "giving in secret."

Fasting and prayer go hand in hand. An old Islamic proverb states that "prayer gets us halfway to heaven, fasting gets us to the door of heaven, and generous alms open the door." Fasting for spiritual purposes goes together with charitable giving for the benefit of the poor. This is an inspired concept. It is designed as a system to take care of the poor and needy. Very few people today, aside from the Latter-day Saints, combine fasting with giving to the poor. We have our monthly fast of two meals (twenty-four hours), and we give to the poor the money that is saved by forgoing those meals. Then we add even more so we can do what President Spencer W. Kimball asked: Give generously several times more than the value of two meals — "much, much more — ten times more." (See Conference Report, April 1974, p. 184.)

Isaiah combines the idea of fasting and almsgiving and blessings. Responding to the rhetorical question "Wherefore have we fasted?" he says: "Is it not to deal thy bread to the hungry, . . . the poor . . . [and] the naked?" (Isaiah 58:3, 7.) We have the promises of our prophets that if the members of the Church will fast, pray, and donate what they save to the fast offering fund, no one in their unit or stake or area will go hungry, naked, or needy. The Lord will provide.

Many individual spiritual and physical blessings result from a monthly fast that is properly begun with a prayer dedicating that fast to the Lord, and ended with a prayer consecrating it to the Lord. Any important decision in one's life should be made after due fasting and prayer. When I have faced the biggest decisions of my life, such as choosing an eternal companion and selecting a discipline to study for my life's profession, I have postponed the making of those decisions until after I have prayed and fasted, and the Lord has blessed me most generously. Of course, I have presented my questions to the Lord, following the pattern outlined in Doctrine and Covenants 9, by studying them out in my mind, making my own decision, and then presenting my request to the Lord for his approval or rejection. Every time I have gone to him in this manner I have received either a quiet, peaceful assurance or a clearly defined no. I cannot say that I have had a "burning bosom" answer except on occasions when I have been sent out to stakes by the Quorum of the Twelve to call a stake president. During these special fasts, impressions are so intimate and personal that they are never presented to the public, and my studying things out through meditation and my making of these supremely important decisions are done in complete secrecy.

Sometimes well-meaning people involve too many other people in their private struggles. I am particularly concerned about young people who take too long to make up their minds about marriage, careers, or jobs and, in effect, discover too late that "the train has pulled out of the station," leaving them behind. Some go through such agony and such long, drawn-out procedures that the Lord may think they are purposely letting others know what they are doing, like the hypocrites — with sad countenances, gloomy looks, play-acting. It is appropriate to ask parents and leaders for guidance and suggestions, but I believe that after we have fasted, pondered the options in our minds, and formed a decision, the Lord wants us to then go to him in secret and our Heavenly Father will reward us in secret. No one need know just how we came to our decision. But I feel that the Lord is impatient with those who are chronically indecisive in deciding to go on a mission now, study for a career now, marry now, and so forth. Some wait too long for a miracle-type message from the Lord, and the opportunity passes them by.

Sister Barbara Winder, former general president of the Relief Society, told Relief Society leaders at an open house sponsored by the Relief Society in March 1990, "Sometimes when someone hears of a family in need or impoverished in a far distant place, that person wants to help—to send food or clothing, make a quilt, pack up books and even send money. One of the problems with this generous response is that while that one family may then be blessed, the neighbors on either side, who are likely in the same situation, will wish that they, too, knew someone who would send relief to them. However, when we respond 'in the Lord's own way,' [giving through the fast offering program], we provide a way for those who have, to give; those who need, to receive; those who receive, to work, if they are able; those who work, to have. It becomes a wonderful cycle that in turn helps people to become self-reliant and thereby able to help others."

The Lord has declared, "It is expedient that I, the Lord, should make every man accountable, as a steward over earthly blessings, which I have made and prepared for my creatures. . . . It is my purpose to provide for my saints, for all things are mine. But it must needs be done in mine own way; . . . this is the way that I, the Lord, have decreed to provide for my saints, that the poor shall be exalted, in that the rich are made low. For the earth is full, and there is enough and to spare; yea, I prepared all things, and have given unto the children of men to be agents unto themselves. Therefore, if any man shall take of the abundance which I have made, and impart not his portion, according to the law of my gospel, unto the poor and the needy, he shall, with the wicked, lift up his eyes in hell, being in torment." (D&C 104:13–18.)

Quoting from Isaiah again, we find an eloquent description of the blessings to be received by those who fast and give to the poor: "Then shall thy light break forth as the morning, and thine health shall spring forth speedily: and thy righteousness shall go before thee; the glory of the Lord shall be thy rereward.

"Then shalt thou call, and the Lord shall answer; thou shalt cry, and he shall say, Here I am. . . .

"And if thou draw out thy soul to the hungry, and satisfy the afflicted soul; then shall thy light rise in obscurity, and thy darkness be as the noonday.

"And the Lord shall guide thee continually, and satisfy thy soul in drought, . . . and thou shalt be like a watered garden, and like a spring of water, whose waters fail not. . . .

"Thou shalt raise up the foundations of many generations; and thou shalt be called the repairer of the breach, the restorer of paths to dwell in." (Isaiah 58:8–12.)

What a blessing!

Paul Anderson has penned the beautiful words of a heartfelt hymn that is a prayer concerning fasting:

> In fasting we approach thee here,
> And pray thy Spirit from above
> Will cleanse our hearts, cast out our fear,
> And fill our hunger with thy love. . . .
>
> And may our fast fill us with care
> For all thy children now in need.
> May we from our abundance share,
> Thy sheep to bless, thy lambs to feed.
>
> This fast, dear Father, sanctify—
> Our faith and trust in thee increase.
> As we commune and testify,
> May we be filled with joy and peace.
> —*Hymns*, no. 139

CHAPTER 13

Treasures, Serving Two Masters, Seeking the Kingdom of God

In the Sermon on the Mount, the Savior now explains that, although we live in a temporal and materialistic world, in order to come unto him we must put temporal things in proper perspective. He takes three concepts in succession. He talks of treasures, but implies that if we seek treasures on earth it will be difficult to follow him. He asks us to choose between God and mammon (defined as the things of this earth, riches, avarice, and worldly gain), for we cannot serve both. And he instructs us to seek first the kingdom of God and his righteousness.

Treasures

Book of Mormon: *"Lay not up for yourselves treasures upon earth, where moth and rust doth corrupt, and thieves break through and steal; but lay up for yourselves treasures in heaven, where neither moth nor rust doth corrupt and where thieves do not break through nor steal. For where your treasure is, there will your heart be also."* (3 Nephi 13:19–21.)

King James Version: *"Lay not up for yourselves treasures upon earth, . . . but lay up for yourselves treasures in heaven, where neither moth nor rust doth corrupt, and where thieves do not break through nor steal: for where your treasure is, there will your heart be also."* (Matthew 6:19–21.)

149

Jerusalem Bible: *"Do not store up treasures for yourselves on earth, where moths and woodworms destroy them and thieves can break in and steal. But store up treasures for yourselves in heaven. . . . For where your treasure is, there will your heart be also."*

Phillips Modern English Bible: *"Don't pile up treasures on earth, where moth and rust can spoil them and thieves can break in and steal. But keep your treasure in Heaven where there is neither moth nor rust to spoil it and nobody can break in and steal. For wherever your treasure is, your heart will be there too!"*

The treasures of the materialistic world—for example, money, property, and possessions such as boats, weekend cabins, trailers and motor homes, television sets, silks and silverware, artworks, and investments—are of only temporary nature, especially when compared to eternal riches that will last forever. When the Lord commanded us to not have any other gods before him, he meant that there should be no priority or obsession or interest for the things of this world over and above the eternal treasures of God.

Edward Bok has said, "Man cannot live by bread alone. The making of money, the accumulation of material power, is not all there is to living. Life is something more than these, and the man who misses this truth misses the greatest joy and satisfaction that can come into his life—service for others." (In Lillian Eichler Watson, ed., *Light from Many Lamps*, p. 19.)

When materialism—the acquisition of riches and earthly treasures—becomes our major priority in life, we will have little time and energy to use in the service to God and to our fellowman, and many will have little time left for their spouse and children. Of infinite value are the treasures of the next life, which mostly center in the eternal family and eternal friendships. If we have ignored those things in this life, we will surely be found wanting in the life to come. Where our treasure is, there will our hearts be also, and the treasures of our hearts should not be the temporary things of this world.

Most people have good intentions, believing that as soon as they have enough of this world's goods to be truly self-sufficient, they can spend more time with the family and in performing church work. But the pursuit of riches is addictive, and it is not easy to free oneself from its grasp. It is not necessarily the possession of riches but our attitude toward them that can put us in jeopardy in inheriting the greatest of all treasures, eternal life. We need to set eternal priorities.

There was a time in my life, when I was a young married man with a new job, working in South America for a prestigious banking firm, when I thought I was wise enough and competent enough to be able to handle the things of the world, as well as my church responsibilities and family obligations. I also justified any material possessions, saying the boat and the airplane were for the family, too. At one time or another, I have owned airplanes, boats, imported and antique cars, and horses. I confess that it took me longer than it should have to realize how much of my attention was being given to these things. The thought came to me that perhaps without realizing it, I could become obsessed with riches and possessions that were easily acquired, and that this obsession could canker and destroy my soul. My spirit reminded me of the Savior's admonition to "lay not up . . . treasures upon earth, . . . for where your treasure is, there will your heart be also." (Matthew 6:19, 21.) I also became aware that if I were so enamored with the material things of this world, the things of most importance in the eternal perspective, including my family and the work of the Lord, would suffer because of my lack of proper attention. I promised the Lord that I would dedicate my time, and everything I had, first to his work and to my family; then I sold those earthly "treasures" and discovered an increase of joy and happiness and contentment. And surprisingly, I learned that my family and I could still enjoy these same amenities, when time permitted, by borrowing planes, boats, horses, and cabins through the generosity of friends who offered! The Lord does not ask that we have no recreational activities, but that we place our priorities in their proper order, concentrating first on the things with paramount eternal importance. I am certain that had I not been willing to make these changes, I would not have been in a position, spiritually, to be useful to the Lord in whatever capacity he desired to use me, wherever or whenever he needed me.

A frequent theme of the Book of Mormon is that those who live the Lord's commandments and seek to follow him will prosper. Many have interpreted this to mean they will prosper as to the things of this world, which is not necessarily true. Couldn't the promise also refer to prospering as to the eternal treasures that we will acquire if our focus is upon doing what the Savior has commanded? However, there is nothing wrong with prosperity, or seeking for riches, as the prophet Jacob taught, *if* it is done for the right reasons and if we use this abundance to alleviate the sufferings and pain of those who are less fortunate. Jacob taught, "Before ye seek for riches, seek ye for the kingdom of God. And after ye have obtained a hope in Christ ye shall obtain riches, if ye seek them; and ye will seek them for the intent to do good—to clothe the naked, and to feed the hungry, and to liberate the captive, and administer relief to the sick and the afflicted." (Jacob 2:18–19.)

Elder Dallin H. Oaks said, "Those who preach the gospel of success and the theology of prosperity are suffering from 'the deceitfulness of riches' (Matthew 13:22) and from supposing that 'gain is godliness' (1 Timothy 6:5). The possession of wealth or the acquisition of significant income is not a mark of heavenly favor, and their absence is not evidence of heavenly disfavor." (*Pure in Heart*, p. 75.) Interestingly, poverty seems to bring an increase of spirituality. In fact, one apostle, who was worrying about the lack of spirituality of some Saints, said, "What they need is a good dose of poverty!"

Elder Boyd K. Packer told us in his conference address in October 1980 that "it is the understanding of almost everyone that success, to be complete, must include a generous portion of both fame and fortune as essential ingredients. . . . We come into mortal life to receive a body and to be tested, to learn to choose. . . . The choice of life is not between fame and obscurity, nor is the choice between wealth and poverty. The choice is between good and evil, and that is a very different matter indeed." (Conference Report, October 1980, pp. 28–29.)

Seeking to build up treasures on earth is a form of covetousness. Paul warned that "the love of money is the root of all evil." (1 Timothy 6:10.) He did not say that money itself is evil—but the *love* of money is. We must be careful that accumulating worldly possessions is not interpreted as being self-reliant, thus excusing ourselves for a misplaced preoccupation with excessively acquiring them. Of course we need to earn a living and have enough skills and education that we can support those who depend upon us, and we need to become self-reliant, but that is far different from trying to get richer or acquire more and more possessions in order to get ahead of or to impress others. Those who covet the wealth or properties of others will certainly suffer spiritually. Greed and covetousness are tools that Satan uses very effectively in corrupting people and turning them from their path of coming unto Christ.

Moroni, in chastening the Nephites because they were "walking in the pride of their hearts," declared: "Ye do love money, and your substance, and your fine apparel, and the adorning of your churches, more than ye love the poor and the needy, the sick and the afflicted. O ye pollutions, ye hypocrites, ye teachers, who sell yourselves for that which will canker, why have ye polluted the holy church of God? Why are ye ashamed to take upon you the name of Christ? Why do ye not think that greater is the value of an endless happiness than that misery which never dies — because of the praise of the world?" (Mormon 8:37–38.)

In the *Church News* editorial for May 19, 1990, we are told that "there are countless ways in which we 'sell' ourselves for money and its adornments and for the praise of the world. One way is by behaving in a manner accepted by the world but not by the Lord. When we are more concerned about what our neighbors or our colleagues or our friends think than by what the Lord might think of us, we sell ourselves 'for that which will canker.'

"Sometimes even what appear to be noble actions are, in the end, worldly pursuits. Fathers, for example, have responsibilities to provide for their families. Sometimes, the hours they must work to do so are long and hard, but the love they have for their families motivates them to continue.

"There are some, however, who work excessively long hours in order to earn more money so that they might provide for their families 'fine apparel' or luxuries of equal or greater value than those of their neighbors. Sometimes these fathers are caught in a vicious cycle: They earn more money so they can buy more things for their families, then their families begin to expect to have those things provided for them in never-ending supply.

"And some mothers are caught in a similar struggle as they walk a fine line between leaving young children in the care of others in order to work outside their home to provide necessities and working to provide what may be luxuries for their families.

"Still, some mothers who have exchanged careers outside their homes for full-time responsibilities in their homes often are entrapped by what they think others think of them. Undue concern for the praise the world heaps upon those who have careers and families jeopardizes the satisfaction and fulfillment that could come through the great work they do within the walls of their homes."

Naturally, we do need to work hard, as the Lord instructed Adam; to be very wise and prudent with our income; and, above all, to avoid the trap of going into debt just to satisfy our selfish desires, since debt brings with it the heavy burden of interest that never sleeps, never takes a vacation, never stops even at night or on weekends. Church leaders are in agreement that a person may need to go into debt to finance a modest home, to finance education and tools of the trade, but that is all — never for speculation and never just to acquire more. Financial burdens can become a cross that is too heavy to bear, and our lives can crumble into pieces — and sometimes we lose those things that matter the most, causing us to suffer spiritually.

"Treasures on earth" are some of the biggest impediments for couples who could be serving missions. They believe that they cannot afford to serve the Lord on a mission because they have to take care of the home they have built, or the cabin in the mountains that might get broken into by thieves, or the motor home they want to travel around in, or the cruise they want to take. After all, they have been working all their lives to acquire these things; they can't be expected to just drop them all to go serve the Lord, can they? That is exactly what the Lord has asked.

Joseph Smith taught that "a religion that does not require the sacrifice of all things never has power sufficient to produce the faith necessary unto life and salvation." (*Lectures on Faith* 6:7.) It is true that if your treasures are on earth you will be reluctant to do those things, such as serving the Lord as missionaries, that lead to earning celestial treasures. The apostle

Paul taught, "Set your affection on things above, not on things on the earth." (Colossians 3:2.) In other words, sell everything, buy a small condominium that can be left alone while you are serving, and go out to serve the Lord. And if everything goes up in smoke or downstream with a flood, the Lord will help you through it somehow. At least you have proven you will serve him, no matter what the cost or sacrifice.

John the Beloved admonished us to "love not the world, neither the things that are in the world. If any man love the world, the love of the Father is not in him. For all that is in the world, . . . the pride of life, is not of the Father, but is of the world. And the world passeth away, . . . but he that doeth the will of God abideth for ever." (1 John 2:15–17.) Forsake the treasures of this world, seek after celestial treasures, and enjoy the fruits of godliness by coming unto Christ.

Serving Two Masters

Book of Mormon: *"No man can serve two masters; for either he will hate the one and love the other, or else he will hold to the one and despise the other. Ye cannot serve God and Mammon."* (3 Nephi 13:24.)

King James Version: *"No man can serve two masters: for either he will hate the one, and love the other; or else he will hold to the one, and despise the other. Ye cannot serve God and mammon."* (Matthew 6:24.)

Jerusalem Bible: *"No one can be the slave of two masters: he will either hate the first and love the second, or treat the first with respect and the second with scorn. You cannot be the slave both of God and of money."*

Phillips Modern English Bible: *"No one can fully serve two masters. He is bound to hate one and love the other, or be loyal to one and despise the other. You cannot serve both God and the power of money."*

We read in *Jesus the Christ* that "those whom the Master was addressing had received of the light of God; the degree of belief they had already professed was proof of that. Should they turn from the great [enterprise] on which they had embarked, the light would be lost, and the succeeding darkness would be denser than that from which they had been relieved. There was to be no indecision among the disciples. No one of them could serve two masters; if he professed so to do he would be an untrue servant to the one or the other. Then followed another profound generalization: 'Ye cannot serve God and mammon.' " (*Jesus the Christ*, 1983, p. 243.)

Being in the world and having to earn enough for our family's needs sometimes places us in a difficult position. Some would even justify their poverty, reasoning that they are more spiritual than those with more. Such comparisons are risky. The Lord expects us to be wise and provident providers. He expects us to be frugal and prudent and good managers. He expects us to work hard, to study well, to develop skills, and to use our gifts and talents. He wants us to be wise stewards over all that he gives to us in this world — to faithfully manage our worldly wealth — so that we can demonstrate to him what kind of stewards and managers we will be over his worlds in the eternities to come. Jesus told us: "If . . . ye have not been faithful in the unrighteous mammon [worldly riches], who will commit to your trust the true riches?" (Luke 16:11.)

I have seen very wealthy Latter-day Saints who put the things of the kingdom first, yet they have been blessed materially because of their vision and skill. We should not be jealous of them nor judge them. I dare say that the ones I am aware of are totally dedicated to the Lord and spiritually oriented, and they certainly have their priorities in order. The moment the Lord wants all they have, they are ready to consecrate it to him. They are not serving mammon but God, and they are ready to make any sacrifice.

At one time in my life I had a difficult choice to make, and I have been much blessed because of the decision my wife and I made. It was a personal test more for my benefit, I think, than for the Lord's. I was finishing my assignment as mission president and had expected to return to international banking, where a good position had been held open for me. A few weeks before being released, however, I was asked to consider employment with the Church at a much lower income, with no significant benefits or future (one cannot be ambitious in Church employment), and to be engaged in a kind of work for which I would have to have additional training. I was not attracted by the offer, and things were not made any easier when I was told that it was not a priesthood call but only a job offer, and that the Church needed to be free to let me go at any time with or without cause, since the job was somewhat of a new experiment to the Church organization. We felt that here was a new test for us. Were we willing to give up the security, prestige, income, fringe benefits, and retirement program of what was then the largest bank in the world, in order to serve the Lord in an obscure and risky position?

After fasting and prayer, my wife and I decided to break ties with the bank and accept employment with the Church. We made our decision, which would change our lives drastically, presented it to the Lord, and received the assurance that we had passed an important test. We had placed serving God over serving our own interests. We have never regretted that decision, and our lives have been enriched in ways that living in a world-oriented environment and atmosphere could never equal. Blessings beyond measure have been showered down upon us and our children. Others may not have to face this kind of decision, but it was necessary for me in order to prove to myself that I could willingly give up a career and a lifestyle that I was thoroughly enjoying.

In his teachings, Christ said that we cannot love two masters (something that controls or dominates our thoughts and actions) for either we will love one and hate the other or we will begin to despise the one and love the other. Service is a powerful master. Elder Marvin J. Ashton has said that we learn to love that which we serve, and we serve that which we love. An example of this truth is the mother who serves her family with barely any thought for herself; the love she has for those whom she serves is beautiful to behold. Elder Ashton describes the effects of service on what we love: "If our top priorities are constantly directed toward the acquisition of more and better worldly goods, it will not take long to increase our love in those directions. . . . How can we decrease our love for things not for our best good? We must . . . stop the expenditure of time and effort in these directions. . . . We must constantly emphasize the truth that we love that to which we give time, whether it be the gospel, God, or gold." (*Ye Are My Friends*, pp. 13–14.)

If we truly want to serve God, we must practice serving him with all our might, mind, and strength. As we serve him, our love for him will increase until our greatest desire will be to focus on doing those things that will please him and our Savior; and, joyfully, we will find ourselves along the path of coming unto Christ, filled with his pure love and approbation.

In the Sermon on the Mount, just after the injunction to not serve two masters and before the commandment to seek first the kingdom, we find instructions from the Savior that have confused many Christians over the centuries. The Book of Mormon account of this instruction was given by the Master to his Twelve Apostles and not to the general membership of the Church. In 3 Nephi we learn more explicitly what the Savior taught: "Jesus . . . looked upon the *twelve* whom he had chosen, and said unto them: . . . Ye are they whom I have chosen to minister unto this people. Therefore I say unto you [to the twelve], take no thought for your life, what ye shall eat, or what ye shall drink. . . . Take no thought, saying, What shall we eat? or, What shall we drink? or, Wherewithal shall we be clothed? For your heavenly Father knoweth that ye have need of all these things." (See 3 Nephi 13:25–32.)

Seeking the Kingdom of God

Book of Mormon: "*Seek ye first the kingdom of God and his righteousness, and all these things shall be added unto you.*" (3 Nephi 13:33.)

King James Version: "*Seek ye first the kingdom of God, and his righteousness; and all these things shall be added unto you.*" (Matthew 6:33.)

Jerusalem Bible: "*Set your hearts on his kingdom first, and on his righteousness, and all these other things will be given you as well.*"

Phillips Modern English Bible: "*Set your heart first on his kingdom and his goodness, and all these things will come to you as a matter of course.*"

Here we have a glorious promise to all who sincerely change the direction of their lives and come unto Christ. Again it is the principle of choosing the proper priorities. When we have been tested in all things until the Lord is certain that we will serve him and seek his kingdom before all else, without regard to the risk or the hazard or sacrifice, then he can truly bless us. We must be motivated by the pure love of Christ in all that we do, however, or we shall surely become hypocrites.

When we experience that mighty change of heart that the prophet Alma speaks of, when we make that spiritual commitment of a broken heart and a contrite spirit, bending our will to our Father's, an eternal bonding takes place between us and the powers of eternity. Our seeking the kingdom of God and his righteousness overpowers any other desire.

The words of the Christian hymn "Come Thou Fount of Every Blessing" express well the attitude we must take:

> Let thy goodness, as a fetter,
> Bind my wandering heart to thee.
> Prone to wander, Lord, I feel it,
> Prone to leave the God I love;
> Here's my heart, O take and seal it;
> Seal it for thy [kingdom] above.

The pioneers who were driven out of Illinois and went west for the gospel's sake gave up sturdy homes and productive farms. These great followers of Christ, their souls burning with the testimony of the truths of the gospel, were seeking first the kingdom of God. They did not seek prosperity in the mountain valleys, but they were blessed spiritually, and today their descendants are reaping those blessings, temporally and spiritually, that their ancestors provided through their obedience, faithfulness, and sacrifice.

As I travel around the stakes of Latin America, I am impressed with the lives and dedication of the Saints. Even in the midst of political and economic problems, those who put the kingdom first and who serve faithfully are prospering more than the people around them. In one country the amount of tithing contributions doubled recently, but with only a few more full-tithe payers than before. The gross national product per capita was decreasing, but the incomes of Saints who paid their tithing were doubling. They were placing the kingdom first, and the Lord was blessing them.

In our day the Lord admonished the Saints: "Seek not for riches but for wisdom, and behold, the mysteries of God shall be unfolded unto you, and then shall you be made rich. Behold, he that hath eternal life is rich." (D&C 6:7.) When we commit ourselves wholly to following the Lord's counsel to seek his kingdom first and endure to the end in righteousness, then we shall be found worthy to hear our Savior declare: "Come, ye blessed of my Father, inherit the kingdom prepared for you from the foundation of the world." (Matthew 25:34.)

Condemn
~~Judge~~ Not
That Ye Be Not ~~Judged~~
condemned

Book of Mormon: *"Judge not, that ye be not judged. For with what judgment ye judge, ye shall be judged; and with what measure ye mete, it shall be measured to you again. And why beholdest thou the mote that is in thy brother's eye, but considerest not the beam that is in thine own eye? Or how wilt thou say to thy brother: Let me pull the mote out of thine eye — and behold, a beam is in thine own eye? Thou hypocrite, first cast the beam out of thine own eye; and then shalt thou see clearly to cast the mote out of thy brother's eye."* (3 Nephi 14:1–5.)

King James Version: *"Judge not, that ye be not judged. For with what judgment ye judge, ye shall be judged: and with what measure ye mete, it shall be measured to you again. And why beholdest thou the mote that is in thy brother's eye, but considerest not the beam that is in thine own eye? Or how wilt thou say to thy brother, Let me pull out the mote out of thine eye; and, behold, a beam is in thine own eye? Thou hypocrite, first cast out the beam out of thine own eye; and then shalt thou see clearly to cast out the mote out of thy brother's eye."* (Matthew 7:1–5.)

Jerusalem Bible: *"Do not judge, and you will not be judged; because the judgments you give are the judgments you will get, and the amount you measure out is the amount you will be given. Why do you observe the splinter in your brother's eye and never notice the plank in your own? How dare you say to your brother, 'Let me take the splinter out of your eye,' when all the time there is a plank in your own? Hypocrite! Take the plank out of your own* eye first, and then you will see clearly enough to take the splinter out of your brother's eye." (Matthew 7:1–5.)

Phillips Modern English Bible: *"Do not criticise people, and you will not be criticised. For you will be judged by the way you criticise others, and the measure you give will be the measure you receive. Why do you look at the speck of sawdust in your brother's eye and fail to notice the plank in your own? How can you say to your brother, 'Let me get the speck out of your eye', when there is a plank in your own? You hypocrite! Take the plank out of your own eye first, and then you can see clearly to remove your brother's speck of dust."*

A favorite hymn of the Latter-day Saints, "Truth Reflects upon Our Senses," refers to the Savior's statement about not judging:

> Truth reflects upon our senses;
> Gospel light reveals to some.
> If there still should be offenses,
> Woe to them by whom they come!
> Judge not, that ye be not judged,
> Was the counsel Jesus gave;
> Measure given, large or grudged,
> Just the same you must receive.
>
> Jesus said, "Be meek and lowly,"
> For 'tis high to be a judge;
> If I would be pure and holy,
> I must love without a grudge.
> It requires a constant labor
> All his precepts to obey.
> If I truly love my neighbor,
> I am in the narrow way.
>
> Once I said unto another,
> "In thine eye there is a mote;
> If thou art a friend, a brother,
> Hold, and let me pull it out."
> But I could not see it fairly,

For my sight was very dim.
When I came to search more clearly,
In mine eye there was a beam.

If I love my brother dearer,
And his mote I would erase,
Then the light should shine the clearer,
For the eye's a tender place.
Others I have oft reproved,
For an object like a mote,
Now I wish this beam removed,
Oh, that tears would wash it out!

Charity and love are healing;
These will give the clearest sight;
When I saw my brother's failing,
I was not exactly right.
Now I'll take no further trouble;
Jesus' love is all my theme;
Little motes are but a bubble
When I think upon the beam.
— *Hymns,* no. 273

Paul made it very clear that God shall render to each of us according to how we treat others. He said, "Thou art inexcusable, O man, whosoever thou art that judgest: for wherein thou judgest another, thou condemnest thyself; for thou that judgest doest the same things. But we are sure that the judgment of God is according to truth against them which commit such things. And thinkest thou this, O man, that judgest them which do such things, and doest the same, that thou shalt escape the judgment of God?" (Romans 2:1–3.)

At a regional conference in Mexico City in May 1988, my wife, Helen, spoke on this sin of criticizing others and judging unrighteously. Here are some of the things she said:

"In the Savior's parable of the unforgiving servant, one of the faults of the servant was that he demanded standards from others that he wasn't prepared to fulfill himself. We're often critical of others but easy on ourselves. We often see clearly the faults of others but find it difficult to see our own. We say we're frank and honest when we speak critically of someone else, but feel offended, claiming that they are unfair, not tolerant or understanding, when others do the same about us. If we fail in anything, we produce half a dozen valid reasons why, which in others would be feeble excuses.

"The important lesson we learn in the parable of the unforgiving servant is that unless and until we have shown forgiveness to our fellowman, we can't receive forgiveness of God.

"One of the major steps we need to take in achieving that goal of being a forgiving person is to first learn not to judge. To be able to keep from judging, there's one principle we need to understand: that each person lives in a 'separate reality,' which means that we all interpret things differently because we each have a different thought system made up of individually unique memories, interpretations, and beliefs.

"Paul taught the importance of accepting differences, without judging, on the occasion of writing to the Romans: 'For one believeth that he may eat all things: another, who is weak, eateth herbs. Let not him that eateth despise him that eateth not; and let not him which eateth not judge him that eateth: for God hath received him. Who art thou that judgest another man's servant? . . . One man esteemeth one day above another: another esteemeth every day alike. Let every man be fully persuaded in his own mind. . . .

" 'Why dost thou judge thy brother? or why dost thou set at nought thy brother? for we shall all stand before the judgment seat of Christ. . . . Every one of us shall give account of himself to God. Let us not therefore judge one another any more: but judge this rather, that no man put a stumblingblock or an occasion to fall in his brother's way.' (Rom. 14:2–13.)

"Everyone does the best they can with what they know. We are much happier when we see the innocence in all behavior and feel compassion or show interest in their point of reference rather than judging. How often do we think, 'How could they possibly be like that, or do that? They would be happier if they would do it my way, like my kind of music, eat the foods I like, treat people the way I think is the right way, etc.' It seems so important to correct others when we think they are wrong, especially those we love.

"Can you imagine what kind of roommates, missionary companions, husbands and wives, parents, brothers and sisters, members of Christ's church we would be if we were more loving, compassionate, and understanding of each other's differences?

"A master gardener does not fret and fume because his roses are not growing into petunias. He simply nurtures all of his flowers with water, weeds them, and gives them fertilizer so they can reach their full potential as roses, petunias, begonias, or whatever they are. We also can simply enjoy and nurture who we and others are rather than destroying our natural capacity to enjoy a beautiful life that is not corrupted with 'shoulds' and 'oughts.' The key is not to judge, but to love and nurture.

"The words of the hymn 'Should You Feel Inclined to Censure' teach us an important lesson regarding finding fault:

> Should you feel inclined to censure
> Faults you may in others view,
> Ask your own heart, ere you venture,
> If you have not failings, too. . . .
> Do not form opinions blindly;
> Hastiness to trouble tends;
> Those of whom we thought unkindly
> Oft become our warmest friends.
> —*Hymns*, no. 235

"I have been guilty of judging — of trying to set right some wrong against me or others, as I perceived it. I then learned how much easier and more fulfilling life is when you let God do the judging. The Lord told us, 'Ye ought to say in your hearts — let God judge between me and thee.' (D&C 64:11.) I learned that a big load is removed from my shoulders when I don't make it my responsibility to be judgmental. So much time and energy is wasted that could be spent on developing tolerance and love for others.

"It is so dangerous to judge and criticize another. We never have all the facts about any situation that would allow us to judge another person righteously for any act or words. We don't have the right to draw our own conclusions based on our limited knowledge, because we really don't understand everything that has gone on to motivate that person's behavior. When we judge, we are looking for the mote in the eye of another, when the beam in our own eye distorts our view. And when we don't forgive, or think we cannot, we destroy that bridge over which we must cross to receive forgiveness.

"Let us have as a daily guide to our conduct the words of Christ when he said: 'Judge not, and ye shall not be judged: condemn not, and ye shall not be condemned: forgive, and ye shall be forgiven.' (Luke 6:37.)"

Our eleventh Article of Faith states: "We claim the privilege of worshiping Almighty God according to the dictates of our own conscience, and allow all men the same privilege, let them worship how, where, or what they may." One element of the commandment to not judge is the admonition to be tolerant and not criticize others for their religious beliefs. Religion is a matter of free agency, and each individual is responsible before God for his or her choice. If we are to follow Christ, we must not be fanatical, critical, or intolerant of others' beliefs. John, the beloved apostle, showed a bit of that tendency when he saw someone casting out devils in the name of Christ. John forbade that person to do works in the name of the Master and reported it to the Savior. Jesus was much more tolerant. He said, "Forbid him not: for there is no man which shall do a miracle in my name, that can lightly speak evil of me. For he that is not against us is on our part." (Mark 9:39–40.)

Lack of tolerance, especially in matters of religion, leads some to want to force their opinions upon others. That was Satan's way, perhaps, because he wanted to forgo free agency and force all to be saved without losing anyone. But force is no solution — not in politics, not in business, and, most important, not in things of the Spirit. There should be only harmony and unity of purpose between those professing different religious beliefs. The pure love of Christ should lead us to love others, no matter what church they belong to, and to truly put into practice in our lives the uplifting principles of tolerance and love that Paul and Moroni taught in their great sermons on charity.

Some of my best friends are members of other churches. During World War II the navy sent me to study for a while at a Catholic university. All of the professors were Jesuit priests, wearing their traditional long black sotanas (habits), and classes began with "Hail Marys" and prayers. I wondered how a lone Mormon boy would fare amid such teachers, but I need not have been concerned. They were polite, kindly men, wise, spiritual, and full of Christian love. I developed a sincere fondness for them and great respect for their sacrifice and dedication. Never did I see an unkind act from any of them — they were living examples of the pure love of Christ.

Prejudice and ignorance lead to intolerance; biases and traditions are deep-seated and difficult to overcome. Nevertheless, anyone with the desire to come unto Christ must overcome these tendencies, not judge anyone in any way, and learn to love and accept each person as brother and sister truly, following the admonition of Paul: "Wherefore receive ye one another, as Christ also received us." (Romans 15:7.)

> Who am I to judge another
> When I walk imperfectly?
> In the quiet heart is hidden
> Sorrow that the eye can't see.
> Who am I to judge another?
> Lord, I would follow thee.
> —*Hymns*, no. 220

Evaluate:

E
Reject – Pity

A
Accept – Admire
→ "Choose the right."

CHAPTER 15

Ask, Seek, Knock

Book of Mormon: "*Ask, and it shall be given unto you; seek, and ye shall find; knock, and it shall be opened unto you. For every one that asketh, receiveth; and he that seeketh, findeth; and to him that knocketh, it shall be opened. Or what man is there of you, who, if his son ask bread, will give him a stone? Or if he ask a fish, will he give him a serpent? If ye then, being evil, know how to give good gifts unto your children, how much more shall your Father who is in heaven give good things to them that ask him?*" (3 Nephi 14:7–11.)

King James Version: "*Ask, and it shall be given you; seek, and ye shall find; knock, and it shall be opened unto you: for every one that asketh receiveth; and he that seeketh findeth; and to him that knocketh it shall be opened. Or what man is there of you, whom if his son ask bread, will he give him a stone? Or if he ask a fish, will he give him a serpent? If ye then, being evil, know how to give good gifts unto your children, how much more shall your Father which is in heaven give good things to them that ask him?*" (Matthew 7:7–11.)

Jerusalem Bible: "*Ask and it will be given to you; search, and you will find; knock, and the door will be opened to you. For the one who asks always receives; the one who searches always finds; the one who knocks will always have the door opened to him. Is there a man among you who would hand his son a stone when he asked for bread? Or would hand him a snake when he asked for a fish? If you, then, who are evil, know how to give your children what is good, how much more will your Father in heaven give good things to those who ask him!*"

170

Phillips Modern English Bible: *"Ask and it will be given to you. Search and you will find. Knock and the door will be opened for you. The one who asks will always receive; the one who is searching will always find, and the door is opened to the man who knocks. If any of you were asked by his son for bread would you give him a stone, or if he asks for a fish would you give him a snake? If you then, for all your evil, quite naturally give good things to your children, how much more likely is it that your Heavenly Father will give good things to those who ask him?"*

In chapter 12 we spoke of the danger of hypocrisy in prayer. In this chapter, we will discuss how to be effective in approaching our Heavenly Father in prayer—how and what we should ask for; how and what we should seek for; and the promises that await those who follow Christ in doing what he commands in this respect.

Prayer is a manifestation of our faith in our Creator. We pray to a God we believe in but cannot see, though we feel that he can hear us at any time of day or night. We believe in a glorious and loving Father in heaven who does not sleep, is not an absentee being, is not a disinterested being, and is not so far away that he cannot care about us or answer us. All of that declaration is a simple statement of faith.

One of my favorite stories in the scriptures is the story about the prophet Elijah and his prayer scene with the priests of Baal. Elijah, perceiving that the people couldn't decide which god to follow—the one and only true Lord God, or Baal—challenged the prophets of Baal to call down fire from heaven. He said, "Call ye on the name of your gods, and I will call on the name of the Lord: and the God that answereth by fire, let him be God." Each was to prepare an altar of stone and place upon it the carcass of an ox. Then they were to each pray to their respective god and ask him to send down fire from heaven to burn up the offering.

The priests of Baal went first. They prayed and prayed. They prayed all day long and nothing happened. Around midday, the prophet began to mock them. He suggested that they pray louder so their god could hear; then he scoffed at them, asking if their god was asleep, thinking that they might try to awaken him. He asked if their god had gone away to meditate or had perhaps gone someplace else to work. The pagan priests prayed harder and harder, louder and louder, without success. Then, to get their god's attention, they began to cut themselves with knives and sharp objects. They bled profusely, but all to no avail.

After a full day of watching the priests of a false god try all their techniques, Elijah took his turn. To show the power of his God, he poured water over the wood under the sacrifice to make the coming miracle even more difficult. Then he prayed, "Lord God of Abraham, Isaac, and of Israel, let it be known this day that thou art God in Israel, and that I am thy servant, and that I have done all these things at thy word. Hear me, O Lord, hear me, that this people may know that thou art the Lord God, and that thou hast turned their heart back again." To the amazement of the pagans, the fire came down and consumed the sacrifice, the wood, and the altar; in fact, it even licked up the water that was in the trench. Elijah was a man of faith. He knew the God to whom he prayed, and the hearts of the people were turned toward the Lord. (See 1 Kings 18.)

In Matthew 7:7–11 we get the impression that a one-time simple "asking" may not be enough. We are told that we should not only ask, but also seek and knock — and do so with faith and diligence. As I read these verses, I have the feeling that we are being told to ask and continue asking, seek and continue seeking, and knock and continue knocking.

A short and simple parable to this effect is told in Luke 11:5–8. Paraphrasing the story, it tells of a neighbor who had unexpected guests arrive late at night. The surprised host was found with no food for his hungry visitors. Even though it was midnight, he knew that his next-door neighbor would help him just as he would help out his neighbor in similar circumstances. He went over and knocked loudly at the door. He called out and told his friend what he needed. The neighbor, sound asleep in bed, with his family also all asleep, first answered, "Don't bother us." The desperate host called out again, insisting that he really needed some bread immediately. The Savior commented that even though the sleeping neighbor would not have arisen just for his friend, he did get up and provide the bread because of the friend's insistence. The Lord was teaching us that we must continue our importuning as long as necessary.

The Lord, who counseled us that "men ought always to pray, and not to faint," also demonstrated this principle in the case of the unjust judge who would not listen to the woman until she had insisted several times. (See Luke 18:1–8.) He wants us to be persistent and not be weary in asking for that which is right. It would be too easy if every prayer were answered the first time it occurred to us to ask. The test of our faith is in our diligence in crying "day and night unto him."

Prayer has been an essential part of the gospel ever since Adam was placed in the Garden of Eden. An angel visited him and declared: "Thou shalt do all that thou doest in the name of the Son, and thou shalt repent and call upon God in the name of the Son forevermore." (Moses 5:8.) Many witnesses throughout the scriptures testify that it is a commandment to call upon the Lord. In modern revelation, given through Joseph Smith in 1831, the Lord declared: "Ye are commanded in all things to ask of God, who giveth liberally; and that which the Spirit testifies unto you even so I would that ye should do in all holiness of heart, walking uprightly before me, considering the end of your salvation, doing all things with prayer and thanksgiving, that ye may not be se-

duced by evil spirits, or doctrines of devils, or the commandments of men." (D&C 46:7.)

To help us in fulfilling his commandments, the Lord has
given us sufficient specific guidelines to follow so that we may
learn how we should ask, what we should ask for, how we
should seek, and what we should seek for.

How We Should Ask

Prophets in both ancient and modern times have given us
guidance on how we should call upon the Lord:

1. *In faith.* Joseph Smith's vision of the Father and the
Son came as a result of his inquiry of the Lord after reading
James 1:5: "If any of you lack wisdom, let him ask of God,
that giveth to all men liberally, and upbraideth not; and it
shall be given him. But let him ask in faith, nothing wavering."

2. *With belief.* In the Book of Mormon Nephi said: "If ye
will not harden your hearts, and ask me in faith, believing
that ye shall receive, with diligence in keeping my commandments, surely these things shall be made known unto
you." (1 Nephi 15:11.)

3. *With sincerity.* In Moroni we are given this counsel: "If
ye shall ask with a sincere heart, having faith in Christ, he
will manifest the truth . . . unto you, by the power of the
Holy Ghost." (Moroni 10:4.)

What We Should (and Should Not) Ask For

We should ask only for that which is right and appropriate.
We are warned that we should "seek not to counsel the Lord,
but to take counsel from his hand." (Jacob 4:10.) "God . . .
doth grant unto you whatsoever ye ask that is right, in faith,
believing that ye shall receive." (Mosiah 4:21.) "Whatsoever
ye ask the Father in my name it shall be given unto you, that
is expedient for you; [but] if ye ask anything that is not expedient for you, it shall turn unto your condemnation." (D&C

88:63–65.) "I know that God will give liberally to him that asketh. Yea, my God will give me, if I ask not amiss." (2 Nephi 4:35.)

Conversely, the scriptures warn us of things we should not ask the Lord for:

1. *"Great things" for ourselves.* "Seekest thou great things for thyself? seek them not: for . . . I will bring evil upon all flesh." (Jeremiah 45:5.)

2. *Signs.* "He that seeketh signs shall see signs, but not unto salvation. . . . Faith cometh not by signs, but signs follow those that believe." (D&C 63:7, 9.)

3. *Worldly possessions.* "Wherefore, seek not the things of this world." (JST Matthew 6:38.)

How We Should Seek

The scriptures teach us how we should approach the Lord:

1. *With prayer and fasting.* "I set my face unto the Lord God, to seek by prayer and supplications, with fasting." (Daniel 9:3.)

2. *Diligently.* "He is a rewarder of them that diligently seek him." (Hebrews 11:6.) "Seek me diligently and ye shall find me." (D&C 88:63.) "The Holy Ghost . . . is the gift of God unto all those who diligently seek him." (1 Nephi 10:17.)

3. *Earnestly.* "Seek ye earnestly the best gifts, always remembering for what they are given." (D&C 46:8.)

4. *In a timely manner.* "O God, . . . early will I seek thee." (Psalm 63:1.) "Seek ye the Lord while he may be found, call ye upon him while he is near." (Isaiah 55:6.)

5. *With all our heart.* "Thou shalt find him, if thou seek him with all thy heart and with all thy soul." (Deuteronomy 4:29.)

What We Should Seek

The Lord has also told us what we should seek:

1. *Wisdom.* "Seek not for riches but for wisdom, and

behold, the mysteries of God shall be unfolded unto you."
(D&C 6:7.)

2. *The kingdom of God.* "Seek the kingdom of God, and
all things shall be added according to that which is just."
(D&C 11:23.) "Before ye seek for riches, seek ye for the
kingdom of God." (Jacob 2:18.) "Seek ye first to build up the
kingdom of God, and to establish his righteousness." (JST
Matthew 6:38.)

3. *Gifts.* "Seek ye earnestly the best gifts, always remembering for what they are given." (D&C 46:8.)

4. *The face of the Lord.* "Seek the face of the Lord always,
that . . . ye shall have eternal life." (D&C 101:38.) "Thy
face, Lord, will I seek." (Psalm 27:8.) "Seek the Lord, and
his strength: seek his face evermore." (Psalm 105:4.) "Seek
his face continually." (1 Chronicles 16:11.)

5. *The gift of the Holy Ghost.* "The Holy Ghost . . . is
the gift of God unto all those who diligently seek him." (1
Nephi 10:17.)

6. *To bring forth Zion.* "Blessed are they who shall seek
to bring forth my Zion." (1 Nephi 13:37.)

7. *Counsel.* "Counsel with the Lord in all thy doings,
and he will direct thee for good." (Alma 37:37.)

8. *Repentance.* "A man sometimes, if he is compelled to
be humble, seeketh repentance; and . . . shall find mercy."
(Alma 32:13.)

9. *Forgiveness.* "As oft as they repented and sought forgiveness, with real intent, they were forgiven." (Moroni 6:8.)

10. *Peace.* "Seek peace, and pursue it." (Psalm 34:14.)

11. *The scriptures.* "Seek ye out of the book of the Lord,
and read." (Isaiah 34:16.)

12. *That which is good.* "Seek good, and not evil, that ye
may live." (Amos 5:14.)

13. *To help others.* "Let no man seek his own, but every
man another's good." (JST 1 Cor. 10:24.)

14. *Those who are less active in the Church.* "If a man have an hundred sheep, and one of them be gone astray, doth he not . . . [seek] that which is gone astray?" (Matthew 18:12.)

15. *The will of the Father.* "I seek not mine own will, but the will of the Father." (John 5:30.)

16. *Glory, honor, and immortality—eternal life.* "[God] will render to every man according to his deeds: to them who by patient continuance in well doing seek for glory and honor and immortality, eternal life." (Romans 2:6–7.)

17. *To edify the Church.* "Seek that ye may excel to the edifying of the Church." (1 Corinthians 14:12.)

Authors Blaine and Brenton Yorgason have written that we must seek righteousness rather than manifestations, explaining: "We must not run faster than we are able, nor demand of the Lord things that, in his wisdom, we have thus far been denied. But does that mean that it is inappropriate to seek to grow spiritually? Of course not! . . . Joseph [Smith] said we are to seek to grow into the principle of revelation, and the Lord told us that we would grow from grace to grace *as we kept the commandments.* . . . Therefore, we do not seek manifestations, but rather we seek righteousness and closeness to the Spirit through obedience and regular repentance." (*Receiving Answers to Prayers,* p. 22.)

Some might ask, "But when I knock, how will I recognize it when he opens? What should I expect? Will he really hear me knock?" We must keep in mind that this promise of the Lord is conditional, just as every other promise is that he has given. Unless we are first obedient and worthy of the companionship of the Holy Ghost, the Lord cannot fulfill his part of the contract. But if we are seeking after righteousness and are counted among those who hunger and thirst to follow the Savior, then we will know for a surety, as Joseph learned in the Sacred Grove, that God truly hears and answers when we call upon him.

How do we recognize his answer? When the Lord spoke to Elijah, it was not in the wind, nor the earthquake, nor the fire, but in a still small voice. (See 1 Kings 19:11–12.) Joseph Smith said: "The Lord cannot always be known by the thunder of His voice, by the display of His glory or by the manifestation of His power. . . . We would say, . . . seek to know God in your closets, call upon him in the fields. Follow the directions of the Book of Mormon, and pray over . . . all things that you possess; ask the blessing of God upon all your labors, and everything that you engage in. . . . Keep the commandments of God; and then you will be able more perfectly to understand the difference between right and wrong—between the things of God and the things of men; and your path will be like that of the just, which shineth brighter and brighter unto the perfect day." (*Teachings of the Prophet Joseph Smith,* p. 247.)

President Harold B. Lee told the Saints: "The fundamental and soul-satisfying step in our eternal quest is to come in a day when each does know, for himself, that God answers his prayers. This will come only after 'our soul hungers,' and after mighty prayer and supplication." (Conference Report, April 1969, p. 133.)

This truth was borne upon the soul of Sister Esperanza Alvarez de Aguilar in a very sacred and spiritual manner during her second pregnancy. The doctor had informed Brother and Sister Aguilar that due to complications, her unborn child was at great risk. They, of course, were alarmed when the doctor gave them two alternatives: have an abortion or give birth to an incomplete and deformed child. "We didn't know what to do," recalled Sister Aguilar. "My husband and I cried, asking ourselves and Heavenly Father why this had happened to us."

One day Sister Aguilar's husband told her, "Heavenly Father knows what we need. If we have a deformed baby as the doctors predict, don't you think we'll love it as much as we would a healthy baby?" Sustained by her husband's faith,

Esperanza agreed they should have the baby, but she was still very fearful.

Then one day, while serving at the Mexico City Temple as an ordinance worker, Esperanza decided to go to the celestial room. Alone in the room, she poured out her feelings in prayer, telling Heavenly Father that she wanted the courage and love necessary to have this child. Suddenly something happened. In her mind and heart these words came to her: "Why should we mourn or think our lot is hard? 'Tis not so; all is right. Why should we think to earn a great reward if we now shun the fight? Gird up your loins; fresh courage take. Our God will never us forsake; And soon we'll have this tale to tell— All is well! All is well!" (*Hymns,* no. 30.)

Sister Aguilar was overcome with a feeling of calm and peace. Turning again to prayer, she expressed gratitude for this immediate and divine response. Though the doctors continued to voice their concerns, the remaining months of the pregnancy passed without complication. Finally the delivery day arrived, and this faithful mother gave birth to a healthy baby girl. "When they showed me my daughter, tears flowed from my eyes," she said. "She was the most beautiful baby I had ever seen. Again I heard in my ears the sweet expression: 'All is well! All is well!' "

May we be counted worthy to receive the glorious promise of the Savior, as John the Beloved revealed to all of us: "And whatsoever we ask, we receive of him, because we keep his commandments, and do those things that are pleasing in his sight." (1 John 3:22.)

The Golden Rule

Book of Mormon: *"All things whatsoever ye would that men should do to you, do ye even so to them, for this is the law and the prophets."* (3 Nephi 14:12.)

King James Version: *"All things whatsoever ye would that men should do to you, do ye even so to them: for this is the law and the prophets."* (Matthew 7:12.)

Jerusalem Bible: *"Always treat others as you would like them to treat you; that is the meaning of the Law and the Prophets."*

Phillips Modern English Bible: *"Treat other people exactly as you would like to be treated by them—this is the meaning of the Law and the Prophets."*

Elder David B. Haight has given us sound counsel concerning our relationship and behavior toward every other human being. He declared: "Someone said, 'We have committed the Golden Rule to memory. May we now commit it to life.' The Savior's teaching, 'Therefore all things whatsoever ye would that men should do to you, do ye even so to them,' should be the basis for all human relationships.

"The Lord is very clear about the conduct He expects from the inhabitants of this earth. Nephi declared: 'And again, the Lord God hath commanded that men should not murder; . . . should not lie; . . . should not steal; . . . should not take the name of the Lord . . . in vain; . . . should not envy; . . . should not have malice; . . . should not contend one with another; . . . should not commit whoredoms; . . . for whoso doeth them shall perish. For none of these iniquities come of the Lord; for he doeth that which is good among the children of men; . . . and . . . inviteth . . . all to come unto him and partake of his goodness' (2 Nephi 26:32–33).

"The time is now to rededicate our lives to eternal ideals and values, to make those changes that we may need to make in our own lives and conduct to conform to the Savior's teachings. From the beginning to the end of His ministry, Jesus asked His followers to adopt new, higher standards in contrast to their former ways. As believers, they were to live by a spiritual and moral code that would separate them not only from the rest of the world but also even from some of their traditions. He asks nothing less of those who follow Him today." (*Ensign*, November 1987, p. 15.)

As Elder Haight explains, the Golden Rule is a summary of the basic philosophy of the Savior as spelled out in the magnificent and timeless Sermon on the Mount. We note that the Savior is trying to help us internalize the commandments so that they come from the intents of the heart and are not just external rules independent from personal righteousness.

In chapter 22 of Matthew we find another version of this all-encompassing law. Though it is expressed differently, it means virtually the same. In the Jerusalem Bible, a title — "the greatest commandment of all" — sets this verse apart. The words from the King James Version are perhaps the most familiar to us: "But when the Pharisees had heard that he had put the Sadducees to silence, they were gathered together. Then one of them, which was a lawyer, asked him a question, tempting him, and saying, Master, which is the great commandment in the law? Jesus said unto him, Thou shalt love the Lord thy God with all thy heart, and with all thy soul, and with all thy mind. This is the first and great commandment. And the second is like unto it, Thou shalt love thy neighbour as thyself. On these two commandments hang all the law and the prophets." (Matthew 22:34–40.)

The Golden Rule means that we should treat others as we want them to treat us; the second part of the "greatest commandment of all" is that we should love our neighbors as ourselves. The similarity between the two commandments is obvious and important. The lawyer, who was undoubtedly an expert in asking questions with hidden traps, was not asking the Savior in order to learn, but to try to embarrass the Lord. Jesus rose to the occasion with a wonderful response by referring to the first and greatest commandment: loving the Lord our God with all our heart, soul, and mind. Our love of God must take precedence over all else and must be the basis for our obedience to every other commandment. Without that love we would never want to make sacrifices or seek to obey to the extent necessary for our salvation. And without the second commandment of loving our fellowmen as we do ourselves, we would never treat our fellowmen as we would want them to treat us.

The Pharisees had listed all the laws and thought they could find some minor points of contradiction between them. The lawyer was hoping to trap Jesus, probably by remembering a law with some interpretation different than that given by the Master. But Jesus' answer was so correct and all-encompassing that there was no room for the lawyer to contradict him.

In his letter to the Romans, Paul tells us that the Golden Rule and the second greatest commandment go together. Paul counsels, "Love one another: for he that loveth another hath fulfilled the law. For this, Thou shalt not commit adultery, Thou shalt not kill, Thou shalt not steal, Thou shalt not bear false witness, Thou shalt not covet; and if there be any other commandment, it is briefly comprehended in this saying, namely, Thou shalt love thy neighbour as thyself." (Romans

13:8–9.) In the Jerusalem Bible, the verse that follows these—
"Love is the one thing that cannot hurt your neighbor; that
is why it is the answer to every one of the commandments"—
leaves no doubt as to how love can purify us.

The Golden Rule and the greatest commandments are
based upon the principle of love. The Savior taught about
love early in his ministry, yet at the Last Supper he returned
to this all-important subject by saying, "A new commandment
I give unto you, That ye love one another." (John 13:34.) In
today's vernacular, he might say, "I give unto you a new
emphasis on an old commandment, Love one another." (See
also John 15 for additional references on love.)

Some authors state that Confucius taught a form of the
Golden Rule twenty-five centuries ago. It was the reversal
from that of the Savior's. He purportedly said: "What you do
not wish done to yourself, do not do to others." These same
experts on ancient religious philosophy point out that Zoroaster taught the same concept in Persia several hundred years
before Confucius. Five hundred years after Confucius, Christ
taught the concept but used it in the positive form we find in
the Bible and the Book of Mormon. Perhaps someday we will
learn that it was also taught in the beginning by Adam and
all the prophets down through the ages. It is a timeless and
an uplifting concept. It is one of those eternal principles that
we recognize as such from the first time we read it.

In a little-known book on developing a Christlike personality we read the following: "What are the important factors
in getting along well with others? The Golden Rule is probably
the basic secret of this art. If we try to give the same thoughtful
consideration to others that we would wish others to give to
us, we shall respect not only their rights but their personalities.
We shall be considerate of their feelings and shall have a real
interest in their welfare. We shall cooperate happily with
others in both work and play. We shall love instead of hate.

We can hate what injures or debases human life without hating the individuals who may be responsible.

"If we truly apply the Golden Rule, we shall try to see ourselves as others see us. We shall thereby become aware of ways in which we are likely to annoy, antagonize, or hurt others. We shall also discover ways in which we may attract others and add to their pleasure and happiness. To develop this ability, we need to learn how to interpret the evidences of others' real attitudes, emotions, and thoughts, as expressed in their behavior. This is more of an art than a science. It is a skill which grows through experience in living with others. Do you enter wholeheartedly into activities for which you make personal sacrifices?

"If we believe in following the Golden Rule we must also believe in the resulting rule or corollary: Sharing wholeheartedly in the experiences of others is the experience of all truly happy, effective personalities." (Bennet and Hand, *Designs for Personality,* pp. 149–51.)

The Straight and Narrow Way

Book of Mormon: *"Enter ye in at the strait gate; for wide is the gate, and broad is the way, which leadeth to destruction, and many there be who go in thereat; because strait is the gate, and narrow is the way, which leadeth unto life, and few there be that find it."* (3 Nephi 14:13–14.)

King James Version: "Enter ye in at the strait gate: for wide is the gate, and broad is the way, that leadeth to destruction, and many there be which go in thereat: because strait is the gate, and narrow is the way, which leadeth unto life, and few there be that find it." (Matthew 7:13–14.)

Jerusalem Bible: *"Enter by the narrow gate, since the road that leads to perdition is wide and spacious, and many take it; but it is a narrow gate and a hard road that leads to life, and only a few find it."*

Phillips Modern English Bible: *"Go in by the narrow gate. For the wide gate has a broad road which leads to disaster and there are many people going that way. The narrow gate and the hard road lead out into life and only a few are finding it."*

There is no doubt that the pathway to come unto Christ is difficult. It is by nature closely defined with strict limits. We cannot waver very far. True, there is always the principle of repentance to aid us in returning to the path, but the path itself is not for the fainthearted.

I have had the experience of trying to pilot a high-performance aircraft down a very narrow electronic pathway through clouds and fog to a runway just barely visible, and only visible at the last moment before touchdown. The radio beam that leads to the runway must be aimed in the right direction so that as I let down through the clouds I will miss mountain peaks, tall buildings, TV antennas, and any other obstacles. I cannot see those obstacles, but I do have faith in the engineers who placed the beam and in the printed guidelines, which tell pilots that if they follow the instructions they will be on the instrument landing path. If I stray to one side or the other I can be in severe danger. If I am too high or too low I will not be able to land correctly and therefore will also be in danger. My speed must be just right at all times. The tolerance for error is very small.

In like manner, the pathway to perfection, which leads us back to the presence of our Heavenly Father and our Savior, is very narrow.

The limits that define the pathway are included in the Sermon on the Mount and in the Ten Commandments. They can also be found in many other places in the scriptures, both ancient and modern, and through the words of the prophets. One of the lists of guidelines that I find most illuminating is located in the table of contents of one of my favorite books, *Christ's Ideals for Living,* compiled by Obert C. Tanner and published by the Church as a Sunday School manual in 1955. To learn if you are close to the path or are straying a bit, just note these chapter topics and measure yourself: faith, humility, courage, purity, reverence, sincerity, temperance, balance, integrity, beauty, truth, serenity, adventure, prayer, self-regard, conviction, endurance, repentance, thanksgiving, joy, love, home, friendship, service, happiness, wealth, brotherhood, peace, justice, mercy, magnanimity, equality, freedom, loyalty, tolerance, progress, forgiveness, trust, worship, steadfastness, sacrifice, and eternal life.

We preach the principles of the restored gospel to all who

will listen. They must decide whether they will follow Christ or not—free agency is an eternal principle that gives each person the right to make choices. President Ezra Taft Benson declared: "Freedom of choice is a God-given eternal principle. The great plan of liberty is the plan of the gospel. There is no coercion about it; no force, no intimidation. A man is free to accept the gospel or reject it. He may accept it and then refuse to live it, or he may accept it and live it fully. But God will never force us to live the gospel. He will use persuasion through His servants. He will call us and He will direct us and He will persuade us and encourage us and He will bless us when we respond, but He will never force the human mind." (*The Teachings of Ezra Taft Benson,* p. 82.) Part of the test of this life is to see whether or not we will seek to follow this straight and narrow path. It is meant to be a thoughtful decision and one that will require obedience and sacrifice. Anything worthwhile requires significant effort.

One path open to us is the pathway described by Christ. The other is the wide and easy road that looks attractive and enticing, but that will lead us carefully down to hell. "Others will he pacify, and lull them away into carnal security, that they will say: All is well in Zion; yea, Zion prospereth, all is well—and thus the devil . . . leadeth them away carefully down to hell." (2 Nephi 28:21.)

Elder Bruce R. McConkie has differentiated for us the meaning of the words *strait* and *straight.* He writes, "The course leading to eternal life is both *strait* and *straight.* It is *straight* because it has an invariable direction—always it is the same. There are no diversions, crooked paths, or tangents leading to the kingdom of God. It is *strait* because it is narrow and restricted, a course where full obedience to the full law is required. Straightness has reference to direction, straitness to width. The gate is *strait;* the path is both *strait* and *straight.*" (*Mormon Doctrine,* p. 769.)

The first requirements for embarking on the straight and strait path are to follow the principles of faith, repentance, and baptism; to receive the Holy Ghost by the laying on of hands; and, for male members of the Church, to be ordained to the Aaronic Priesthood and then to the Melchizedek Priesthood. The pathway becomes even more narrow when we add the qualifications needed to participate in the saving ordinances of the temple endowment and the eternal sealing of husband and wife. But this is not all: after complying with all this, after experiencing the mighty change of heart that causes one to no longer do things that are displeasing to Heavenly Father, we must continue in obedience, hungering and thirsting after righteousness, enduring to the end, doing good for God and to all people, in order to be worthy to enter back into the presence of our Heavenly Father and his Son, Jesus Christ.

One of the best scriptural descriptions of the path — of both finding it and staying on it — is in Nephi's powerful sermon in chapter 31 of 2 Nephi. Early in this chapter the prophet repeats several times that we must follow Christ, come unto him, and take his name upon us. Then we read the following: "The gate by which ye should enter is repentance and baptism by water; and then cometh a remission of your sins by fire and by the Holy Ghost. And then are ye in this strait and narrow path which leads to eternal life; yea, ye have entered in by the gate; ye have done according to the commandments of the Father and the Son . . . unto the fulfilling of the promise which he hath made, that if ye entered in by the way ye should receive." (2 Nephi 31:17–18.)

Referring to Nephi's declaration, Larry Dahl, an LDS scholar, has written: "This is a sobering thought! With what it takes to get to that point, one might wish it were near the end of the path to eternal life, rather than the very beginning. But Nephi's point is clear: 'And *then* are ye in this strait and narrow path which leads to eternal life; yea, ye have entered in by the gate.' . . . Nephi asks then answers the next obvious question: 'And now, my beloved brethren, after ye have gotten into this strait and narrow path, I would ask if all is done? Behold, I say unto you, Nay; for ye have not come thus far save it were by the word of Christ with unshaken faith in him, relying wholly upon the merits of him who is mighty to save.' . . . The essence of this response seems to be that the credit for our getting through the gate and onto the strait and narrow path belongs to Christ, not us, but that *now we must* rely appropriately upon our own merit, and not depend 'wholly' upon the merit of Christ. We must demonstrate that our change of heart is permanent, that our commitment to obey is stronger than the enticements of the world and the devil, and we must do this day after day, year after year, . . . through good times and bad." (*The Book of Mormon: Second Nephi, the Doctrinal Structure,* pp. 368–69.)

Christ said, "I am the way, the truth, and the life: no man cometh unto the Father, but by me." (John 14:6.) In declaring this, he is also telling us that no other way, no other road, no other system, no other name will bring salvation. The old saying "All roads lead to Rome" is a statement that is not true when applied to the pathway to eternal life. Christ declared, "I am the door [or gate]: by me if any man enter in, he shall be saved." (John 10:9.)

When the Savior says that he is the door, the gate, the path, he is not saying that he is a parallel route or that he is an alternate route. He is most emphatic when he states that he is the *only* way. Therein lies the major choice of this life. We must find Christ. We must come unto him in the way that he has commanded. There will always be those who say they need more freedom, or that commandments are old-fashioned, or that in this modern day of men on the moon and stations in space we should not be so strict with commandments and doctrines and ordinances or insist that they be performed exactly the same way as they were two thousand years ago. The Savior himself says, however, that his way is the *only* way—it is his way then and now. If we desire the blessings that are promised to the obedient, we must make the choice to follow him and not procrastinate or waver.

The straight and narrow way by which we can walk toward godliness is contrasted with the broad highway leading to destruction. The attractions of the world are many, the temptations of Satan to detour us are myriad, but if we are willing to make the decision to follow Christ, then he will walk with us and show us the way. And because of what the Lord has revealed through his prophets, we will be able to chart our course accurately. Whenever he calls and asks, as he asked Adam, "Where art thou?" (Genesis 3:9), we will be able to answer without difficulty or hesitation, "Here am I, Father, following the pathway to thee."

To do so, we must, as King Benjamin declared in his temple sermon, "[yield] to the enticings of the Holy Spirit, [put] off the natural man and . . . [become] as a child, submissive, meek, humble, patient, full of love, willing to submit to all things which the Lord seeth fit to inflict upon [us], even as a child doth submit to his father." (Mosiah 3:19.)

Beware of False Prophets

Book of Mormon: *"Beware of false prophets, who come to you in sheep's clothing, but inwardly they are ravening wolves. Ye shall know them by their fruits. . . . Every good tree bringeth forth good fruit; but a corrupt tree bringeth forth evil fruit."* (3 Nephi 14:15–20.)

King James Version: *"Beware of false prophets, which come to you in sheep's clothing, but inwardly they are ravening wolves. Ye shall know them by their fruits. . . . Even so every good tree bringeth forth good fruit; but a corrupt tree bringeth forth evil fruit."* (Matthew 7:15–20.)

Jerusalem Bible: *"Beware of false prophets who come to you disguised as sheep but underneath are ravenous wolves. You will be able to tell them by their fruits. . . . A sound tree produces good fruit but a rotten tree bad fruit."*

Phillips Modern English Bible: *"Be on guard against false religious teachers, who come to you dressed up as sheep but are really greedy wolves. You can tell them by their fruits. . . . Every good tree produces sound fruit, but a rotten tree produces bad fruit."*

We believe in the same organization that existed in the primitive church of Christ, and that includes the principle of being led by a living prophet accompanied and supported by counselors and apostles whom we sustain as prophets, seers, and revelators. Our message to the world is to "come unto Christ" by following a living prophet who speaks for God in these modern days just as in times of old. "Surely the Lord

God will do nothing, but he revealeth his secret unto his servants the prophets." (Amos 3:7.)

The tribes of Israel believed in true prophets for many centuries, and even today the Jews continue to believe in the words of the ancient prophets of the Old Testament. But they stopped being led by prophets with the close of the Old Testament. The book of Malachi, which is the last book in the Old Testament, was probably written about the middle of the fifth century before Christ. Other accounts in the Old Testament may have been written after that—the books of Joel and Jonah, for example, usually being dated in the fourth century B.C.—but modern Judaism does not follow modern prophets as the people of Israel followed God's prophets in the days of old.

The Islamic religion accepts all Israelite and Christian prophets, including Christ, but only as a prophet and not as the very Son of God. They have their own prophet, Mohammed, who died in the year A.D. 632, and they believe that he was the last of God's prophets on earth.

The majority of Christians accept and preach the words of the prophets as found in both the Old and the New Testament, but have not been led by living prophets since that time, nor do they accept the possibility that there are prophets upon the earth again today. The Church of Jesus Christ of Latter-day Saints is the only Christian religion that claims to be led by a living prophet. It is one of the unique and distinctive principles of our religion.

In this discussion, however, we will discuss how to identify *false* prophets. It is not easy to describe a false prophet because, by design, the false prophet is trying to deceive. The Prophet Joseph Smith wrote, "When a man goes about prophesying, and commands men to obey his teachings, he must either be a true or false prophet. False prophets always arise to oppose the true prophets and they will prophesy so very near the truth that they will deceive almost the very chosen ones." (*Teachings of the Prophet Joseph Smith*, p. 365.)

The Prophet also gave us this advice regarding false prophets: "If any person should ask me if I were a prophet, I should not deny it, as that would give me the lie; for, according to John, the testimony of Jesus is the spirit of prophecy; therefore, if I profess to be a witness or teacher, and have not the spirit of prophecy, which is the testimony of Jesus, I must be a false witness; but if I be a true teacher and witness, I must possess the spirit of prophecy, and that constitutes a prophet; and any man who says he is a teacher or preacher of righteousness, and denies the spirit of prophecy, is a liar, and the truth is not in him; and by this key false teachers and impostors may be detected." (*Teachings*, p. 269.)

One of the finest works I have ever read on the subject of false prophets and the distinctive qualities of true prophets is the masterpiece by Hugh Nibley, *The World and the Prophets*. He writes: "The regular scriptural term to describe the leaders of all unauthorized congregations is *false prophets*. The fatal defect of such congregations is that they are led by false prophets, and we are told that these would abound in the earth, all claiming to be followers of Christ.

"What is a false prophet? He is one who usurps the prerogatives and the authority which by right belong only to a prophet of God. The false prophet need not claim to be a prophet, indeed, most false prophets do not believe in prophecy or even in God, nor do they want anyone else to. Those who would lead the Russians into the promised land are plainly false prophets, but how much faith do they put in prophecy? The . . . term 'pseudo-prophet' designates one who is not a prophet, but who occupies the place that rightly belongs to a prophet, regardless of whether he has been put there by himself or by his followers. Fool's gold, the glittering yellow pyrites that one finds sometimes on the beach, is so called not because *it* pretends to be gold, but because fools take it for gold. A pseudo-prophet is one to whom foolish people accord the obedience and attention due only a true prophet, whether he or they actually take him for a prophet or not.

"Even good, devout, sincere men and women can be false prophets. We can illustrate this point by recalling the attitude of Socrates toward his friends Gorgias, Protagoras, and other great Sophists. He respected and admired them for their powerful minds, their moral fervor, and their sincere desire to improve the character and the minds of youth. Yet for all that, these men were, in Socrates' opinion, dangerous deceivers, all of them, for they were teachers of false doctrine. Socrates did not consider himself qualified to guide the lives of his fellows; all his life he sought for one so qualified—what he was looking for was a prophet, as Professor Jaeger has indicated in the case of his disciples—and when he insisted that he had never found such a man, and that those who thought themselves most qualified were even less worthy than he, his boldness cost him his life. His pupil Plato poked fun at the way the Sophists accepted the worshipful adulation of the multitude and of their disciples, for nothing disturbed him more than the incurable tendency of the schools to make false prophets out of good men. By his standard we still live in a world of false prophets. Anyone whose work competes with God's work, who makes claims on the time and energies of men which rightly belong to God, who puts the word of God in second place to the theories of men, or forces the teachings of true prophets to yield precedence to his own discourses—anyone, in a word, who puts his own knowledge above or on a level with revelation from heaven is a false prophet." (*The World and the Prophets*, vol. 3 of the Collected Works of Hugh Nibley, p. 254.)

Paul, in writing to the Corinthians, described some of the ruses used by Satan and his followers and warned that "such are false apostles, deceitful workers, transforming themselves into the apostles of Christ. And no marvel; for Satan himself is transformed into an angel of light. Therefore it is no great thing if his ministers also be transformed as the ministers of righteousness; whose end shall be according to their works." (2 Corinthians 11:13–15.)

In defense of living prophets, Dr. Nibley said: "In the realm of the mind, in letters, the arts, and in most of the sciences, it was the ancient Greeks, most educated people will concede, who walked off with nearly all the first prizes. It is hard to say anything on any but the most specialized and technical of matters that some Greek many centuries ago did not say better. If any people ever knew and lived life well and fully, it was the chosen spirits among the Greeks. They explored every avenue of human experience; they inquired into every possibility of broadening and improving the mind; they sought the truth as persistently and as honestly as men can ever be expected to seek; and, sounding the depths and skirting the outmost bounds of man's wisdom, came to the unanimous conclusion that the wisdom of man is as nothing.

"The man to whom the Greeks themselves always gave first place among their wisest, Solon of Athens, sums up his own experience in unambiguous elegiacs:

" 'Like gaping fools we amuse ourselves with empty dreams. . . . Do not doubt it, insecurity follows all the works of men, and no one knows, when he begins an enterprise, how it will turn out. One man, trying his best to do the right thing, steps right into ruin and disaster, because he cannot see what is ahead; while another behaves like a rascal and not only escapes the penalty of his own folly but finds himself blessed with all kinds of success.'

"The greatest of their lyric poets told the Greeks in one of his greatest odes [that] 'the hopes of men are often exalted in one moment only to be dashed down in the next, as they roll helplessly in a sea of false expectations and miscalculations. For no mortal man ever got an absolute guarantee from the gods that his affairs would turn out as he thinks they would. There is always some unknown quantity that vitiates any attempt to predict the future.' . . .

"The early Christian apologists made use of this confessed limitation of the wisest pagans, this fatal obstacle not only to human perfection but even to the enjoyment of a few brief hours and weeks of unsullied happiness, to display what they regarded as the peculiar advantage of their own religion. 'Neither by nature nor by any human skill,' wrote Justin Martyr to the Greeks, 'is it possible for men to know such high and holy things; but only by a gift that descends from above upon holy men from time to time.' Justin explains elsewhere that these men are called prophets and are a type of human entirely unknown to the heathen world. 'They do not need training in speech or skill in controversy and argument,' he continues here, 'but only to keep themselves pure to receive the power of the Spirit of God, so that the divine plectrum can express itself through them as on the strings of a lyre, making use of righteous men and revealing to them the knowledge of sacred and heavenly things. Wherefore they all speak as with a single mouth and a single tongue . . . concerning all things which is needful for us to know. . . . The fact that they all agree, though speaking at widely separated times and places, is the proof of their divinity.'

"Note the interesting musical analogy of sympathetic vibrations. The holy men can receive God's revelations because they are in tune to the proper wave length, so to speak. God can play on them as a plectrum plucks the strings of a lyre because they are prepared to vibrate to his touch—not by virtue of any special training, and not whenever *they* choose to respond, but whenever it pleases God 'from time to time,' to move them from heaven. Such is the nature of the prophetic gift, says Justin. The early Christians felt that without this gift of direct revelation from heaven such as is received only by prophets, they would be no better than the heathen — well-meaning but bankrupt. . . .

"But must the church always have *living* prophets in its midst? Is it not enough that we have the words of the prophets of old preserved in holy writ? The answer to that is clear enough in the few passages we have cited. The true church must and will always have living prophets. But that is un-welcome news to the world. It has always been poison. It is the one teaching that has made the restored gospel unacceptable to the wisdom of men. A *dead* prophet the world dearly desires and warmly cherishes; he is a priceless tradition, a spiritual heritage, a beautiful memory. But woe to a living prophet! He shall be greeted with stones and catcalls even by pious people. The men who put the Apostles to death thought they were doing God a favor, and the Lord tells us with what reverence and devotion men adorn the tombs of the prophets whom they would kill if they were alive.

"Men can read the words of a dead prophet and apply his heavy charges to that dead generation to which the prophet spoke, piously shaking their heads the while and repeating, 'If we had been in the days of our fathers, we would not have been partakers with them in the blood of the prophets.' . . .

"Here we have something in the nature of a general principle. The rejection of living prophets and the veneration of dead ones is not a folly limited to one nation or to one generation. It meets us throughout the long history of Israel as a sort of standard procedure. Nor did it cease with the coming of Christ, who promised his disciples that they would be treated as badly and rejected as completely as he. . . .

"It was a test that few have ever passed: the humiliating test of recognizing a true prophet and taking instruction from the weak and humble things of the earth. Was the wondrous modern age of applied science that began in the nineteenth century to be excused from taking the same test of authority? Remember that the prophets of old came to generations that were very modern in their thinking, smart and sophisticated, advanced, liberated, intellectual; the Hellenistic world, if any-thing, surpassed our own in those qualities of social advance-ment. But to come to our own age, do you think the God of heaven is going to come unannounced by prophets? God's declared policy of testing the world by the sending of prophets from time to time was not abrogated two thousand years ago. Men have not so changed, and God has not so changed but that this sure touchstone of past ages can be employed with full effect in our own day. It is precisely those ages which think themselves beyond such things that are most eligible for the warning voice of the prophets. Our message is that God has called prophets again in these days and that the world might well heed their words." (*The World and the Prophets*, pp. 1–3, 5–7.)

In modern revelation we read, "The voice of the Lord is unto the ends of the earth, that all that will hear may hear: . . . and the arm of the Lord shall be revealed; and the day cometh that they who will not hear the voice of the Lord, neither the voice of his servants, neither give heed to the words of the prophets and apostles, shall be cut off from the people." (D&C 1:11, 14.)

He That Doeth
the Will of My Father

Book of Mormon: *"Not every one that saith unto me, Lord, Lord, shall enter into the kingdom of heaven; but he that doeth the will of my Father who is in heaven. Many will say to me in that day: Lord, Lord, have we not prophesied in thy name, and in thy name have cast out devils, and in thy name done many wonderful works? And then will I profess unto them: I never knew you; depart from me, ye that work iniquity."* (3 Nephi 14:21–23.)

King James Version: *"Not every one that saith unto me, Lord, Lord, shall enter into the kingdom of heaven; but he that doeth the will of my Father which is in heaven. Many will say to me in that day, Lord, Lord, have we not prophesied in thy name? and in thy name have cast out devils? and in thy name done many wonderful works? And then will I profess unto them, I never knew you: depart from me, ye that work iniquity."* (Matthew 7:21–23.)

Jerusalem Bible: *"It is not those who say to me, 'Lord, Lord,' who will enter the kingdom of heaven, but the person who does the will of my Father in heaven. When the day comes many will say to me, 'Lord, Lord, did we not prophesy in your name, cast out demons in your name, work many miracles in your name?' Then I shall tell them to their faces: I have never known you; away from me, you evil men!"*

Phillips Modern English Bible: *"It is not everyone who keeps saying to me 'Lord, Lord' who will enter the kingdom of Heaven,* *but the man who actually does my Heavenly Father's will. In 'that day' many will say to me, 'Lord, Lord, didn't we preach in your name, didn't we cast out devils in your name, and do many great things in your name?' Then I shall tell them plainly, 'I have never known you. Go away from me, you have worked on the side of evil!' "*

Referring to the subject of doing the will of the Father, Elder James E. Talmage wrote: "Religion is more than the confession and profession of the lips. . . . Only by doing the will of the Father is the saving grace of the Son obtainable. To assume to speak and act in the name of the Lord without the bestowal of authority, such as the Lord alone can give, is to add sacrilege to hypocrisy. Even miracles wrought will be no vindication of the claims of those who pretend to minister in the ordinances of the gospel while devoid of the authority of the Holy Priesthood." (*Jesus the Christ*, 1983, p. 229.)

Since Elder Talmage affirms that this scripture is about authority, let us read what Elder Bruce R. McConkie said about this important principle. "As pertaining to eternity, priesthood is the eternal power and authority of Deity by which all things exist; by which they are created, governed, and controlled; by which the universe and worlds without number have come rolling into existence; by which the great plan of creation, redemption, and exaltation operates throughout immensity. It is the power of God.

"As pertaining to man's existence on this earth, priesthood is the power and authority of God delegated to man on earth to act in all things for the salvation of men. It is the power by which the gospel is preached; by which the ordinances of salvation are performed so that they will be binding on earth and in heaven." (*Mormon Doctrine*, p. 594.)

I had an interesting gospel conversation about priesthood authority with a client in my bank office many years ago. After discussing business matters, we turned to religion. We had enough confidence in our friendship that we could each discuss the other's religious beliefs and still maintain both our friendship and our business relationship. When I asked, "Where do you find your priesthood authority, since the Catholic church excommunicated the founders of your religion?" he responded that authority was not needed nor was it the issue — the issue was the saving grace of Christ.

I had previously heard how Elder Hugh B. Brown handled a similar discussion when he was in military service, so I used the same approach. I pulled from my drawer a form the bank used to advise the appropriate departments that credit had been approved and funds could then be deposited to a client's account. Showing my friend the form, I said, "You can write better than I can. Why don't you approve a million dollar loan to your company? Sign it there where my signature usually goes; then take it to the head teller. Do you think he will give you the funds?"

"Of course not," he replied.

"Why not?"

"Well, in the first place, your head teller would know that amount is way too large for my small company to merit, and he would then look at the signature and would know either that it was forged, or . . . " He paused.

I asked, "Yes . . . go on . . . or what?"

"I get the point. He would know that I did not have the authority that you have to approve a loan."

I smiled and said, "You're a hundred percent right! If authority is needed to approve a loan, then why is not authority needed to promise someone blessings in this life and in the life to come?"

The sacred authority of the priesthood of the Son of God is not given to those who merely ask for it. Paul taught that "no man taketh this honour unto himself, but he that is called of God, as was Aaron." (Hebrews 5:4.) Any ordinances performed without that authority are as invalid as a forged signature on a loan. Many baptisms and confirmations and other ordinances are performed by well-meaning people, but if those people lack the proper authority, they have no promise that the ordinance will be validated in this or the next life. Many, we fear, will be disillusioned when they arrive on the other side and find that the ordinances performed for them were invalid and the authority those who performed the ordinances thought they had is nonexistent. Sincerity or faith alone is not enough.

Elder James E. Talmage taught the following concerning authority: "We claim that the authority to administer in the name of God is operative in The Church of Jesus Christ of Latter-day Saints today; and that this power or commission was conferred upon the first officers of the Church by ordination under the hands of those who had held the same power in earlier dispensations. That the authority of the holy priesthood was to be taken from the earth as the apostles of old were slain, and that of necessity it would have to be restored from heaven before the Church could be reestablished, may be shown by scripture. On May 15, 1829, while Joseph Smith and Oliver Cowdery were engaged in earnest prayer for instruction concerning baptism for the remission of sins, mention of which Joseph Smith had found in the plates from which he was then engaged in translating the Book of Mormon, a messenger from heaven descended in a cloud of light. He announced himself as John, called of old the Baptist, and said he had come under the direction of Peter, James, and John, who held the keys of the higher Priesthood. The angel laid his hands upon the two young men and ordained them to authority, saying: 'Upon you my fellow servants, in the name of Messiah I confer the Priesthood of Aaron, which holds the keys of the ministering of angels, and of the gospel of repentance, and of baptism by immersion for the remission of sins;

and this shall never be taken again from the earth, until the sons of Levi do offer again an offering unto the Lord in righteousness.' [D&C 13.]

"A short time after this event, Peter, James, and John appeared to Joseph Smith and Oliver Cowdery, and ordained the two to the higher or Melchizedek Priesthood, bestowing upon them the keys of the apostleship, which these heavenly messengers had held and exercised in the former Gospel dispensation. This order of Priesthood holds authority over all the offices in the Church, and includes power to administer in spiritual things; consequently all the authorities and powers necessary to the establishment and development of the Church were by this visitation restored to earth." (*Articles of Faith,* 1985, pp. 170–71.)

Rote ceremonies, mechanical worshiping, and vain repetition do not produce personal salvation. The case of the Pharisee, a man who did everything according to the laws of the Jews and who was greatly honored by the community, and the publican, who collected customs duties and taxes and had a reputation for accepting bribes, illustrates this principle: "Two men went up into the temple to pray; the one a Pharisee and the other a publican. The Pharisee stood and prayed thus with himself, God, I thank thee, that I am not as other men are, extortioners, unjust, adulterers, or even as this publican. I fast twice in the week, I give tithes of all that I possess. And the publican, standing afar off, would not lift up so much as his eyes unto heaven, but smote upon his breast, saying, God be merciful to me a sinner."

Then, we are told, Christ said, "I tell you, this [second] man went down to his house justified [blessed by God] rather than the other; for every one that exalteth himself shall be abased; and he that humbleth himself shall be exalted." (Luke 18:10–14.)

One of the main requirements of this lesson of the Savior's

is that we put our religion into practice by performing righteous acts and by obeying his commandments faithfully—we should be participants and not spectators. James taught, "Lay apart all filthiness and superfluity of naughtiness, and receive with meekness the engrafted word, which is able to save your souls. But be ye doers of the word, and not hearers only, deceiving your own selves. For if any be a hearer of the word, and not a doer, he is like unto a man beholding his natural face in a glass: for he beholdeth himself, and goeth his way, and straightway forgetteth what manner of man he was." (James 1:21–24.)

James also explained, "What doth it profit, my brethren, though a man say he hath faith, and have not works? can faith save him? . . . Faith, if it hath not works, is dead, being alone. . . . Shew me thy faith without thy works, and I will shew thee my faith by my works. . . . Faith without works is dead." (James 2:14, 17–18, 26.)

Some tend to think that just because a few ordinances have been performed, or just because they have repented, they can relax and think they "have it made." This life is not one of arrival; rather it is a journey, where we are continually being given the opportunity to prove ourselves worthy of the rewards promised to those whose efforts have been characterized with steadfastness, hope, faith, and love throughout life to the very last moment of this existence.

Nephi said, "And now, my beloved brethren, after ye have gotten into this strait and narrow path, I would ask if all is done? Behold, I say unto you, Nay; for ye have not come thus far save it were by the word of Christ with unshaken faith in him, relying wholly upon the merits of him who is mighty to save.

"Wherefore, ye must press forward with a steadfastness in Christ [total commitment], having a perfect brightness of hope [faith and hope cannot be separated], and a love of God and of all men [always seeking to serve and help others]. Wherefore, if ye shall press forward, feasting upon the word of Christ [studying the scriptures and other words of the prophets — past and present], and endure to the end, behold, thus saith the Father: Ye shall have eternal life.

"And now, behold, my beloved brethren, this is the way; and there is none other way nor name given under heaven whereby man can be saved in the kingdom of God. And now, behold, this is the doctrine of Christ, and the only and true doctrine of the Father, and of the Son, and of the Holy Ghost." (2 Nephi 31:19–21.)

The Lord also will declare "I never knew you" to those who, even after many "good" deeds, are found wanting as the scribes and Pharisees were. Elder Dallin H. Oaks of the Council of the Twelve has written concerning motives for righteous acts: "Jesus looked beyond the actions of the scribes and Pharisees and condemned them because of their motives. He likened them to 'whited sepulchres,' which appear beautiful outside but are unclean inside. Although their actions he referred to were appropriate, they were acting for the wrong reasons. 'Even so ye also outwardly appear righteous unto men,' he told them, 'but within ye are full of hypocrisy and iniquity' (Matthew 23:27–28). In contrast, in choosing his disciples Jesus praised Nathanael as 'an Israelite indeed, in whom is no guile' (John 1:47)." (*Pure in Heart*, p. 4.)

If we are like the hypocrites, professing to do righteous deeds such as giving to the poor, serving our fellowmen, taking care of the sick, and so on, but doing them to impress others instead of because we really want to do the Lord's will, the Savior will not accept our works. There is ample scriptural evidence that teaches us that in order to obtain blessings by these good acts, we must have the proper motive for doing them. Mormon taught: "God hath said a man being evil cannot do that which is good; for if he offereth a gift, or prayeth unto

God, except he shall do it with real intent it profiteth him nothing. For behold, it is not counted unto him for righteousness." (Moroni 7:6–7.)

In our day the Lord has declared: "Although a man [even someone who has been given proper authority to act in God's name] may have many revelations, and have power to do many mighty works, yet if he boasts in his own strength, and sets at naught the counsels of God, and follows after the dictates of his own will and carnal desires, he must fall and incur the vengeance of a just God upon him." (D&C 3:4.)

Our greatest desire should be to obey the Lord's commands, follow after him, and want to make his will our will—and then to act according to this desire. The prophet Alma's advice to his son Corianton is explicit: "It is requisite with the justice of God that men should be judged according to their works; and if their works were good in this life, and the desires of their hearts were good, . . . they should also, at the last day, be restored unto that which is good." (Alma 41:3.)

CHAPTER 20

Build upon the Rock

Book of Mormon: *"Therefore, whoso heareth these sayings of mine and doeth them, I will liken him unto a wise man, who built his house upon a rock—and the rain descended, and the floods came, and the winds blew, and beat upon that house; and it fell not, for it was founded upon a rock. And every one that heareth these sayings of mine and doeth them not shall be likened unto a foolish man, who built his house upon the sand—and the rain descended, and the floods came, and the winds blew, and beat upon that house; and it fell, and great was the fall of it."* (3 Nephi 14:24–27.)

King James Version: *"Therefore whosoever heareth these sayings of mine, and doeth them, I will liken him unto a wise man, which built his house upon a rock: and the rain descended, and the floods came, and the winds blew, and beat upon that house; and it fell not: for it was founded upon a rock. And every one that heareth these sayings of mine, and doeth them not, shall be likened unto a foolish man, which built his house upon the sand: and the rain descended, and the floods came, and the winds blew, and beat upon that house; and it fell: and great was the fall of it."* (Matthew 7:24–27.)

Jerusalem Bible: *"Therefore, everyone who listens to these words of mine and acts on them will be like a sensible man who built his house on rock. Rain came down, floods rose, gales blew and hurled themselves against that house, and it did not fall: it was founded on rock. But everyone who listens to these words of mine and does not act on them will be like a stupid man who built his house on sand. Rain came down, floods rose, gales blew and struck that house, and it fell; and what a fall it had!"*

Phillips Modern English Bible: *"Everyone then who hears these*

words of mine and puts them into practice is like a sensible man
who builds his house on rock. Down came the rain and up came
the floods, while the winds blew and roared upon that house—and
it did not fall because its foundations were on rock. And everyone
who hears these words of mine and does not follow them can be
compared with a foolish man who built his house on sand. Down
came the rain and up came the floods, while the winds blew and
battered that house till it collapsed, and fell with a great crash."

Elder James E. Talmage, in his closing comments on the
Sermon on the Mount in *Jesus the Christ*, wrote: "The Sermon
on the Mount has stood through all the years since its delivery
without another to be compared with it. No mortal man has
ever since preached a discourse of its kind. The spirit of the
address is throughout that of sincerity and action, as opposed
to empty profession and neglect. In the closing sentences the
Lord showed the uselessness of hearing alone, as contrasted
with the efficacy of doing. The man who hears and acts is
likened unto the wise builder who set the foundation of his
house upon a rock; and in spite of rain and hurricane and
flood, the house stood. He that hears and obeys not is likened
unto the foolish man who built his house upon the sand; and
when rain fell, or winds blew, or floods came, behold it fell,
and great was the fall thereof." (*Jesus the Christ*, 1983, pp.
229–30.)

Elder Joseph B. Wirthlin of the Council of the Twelve
wrote on the subject of building upon the rock for an article
in the *New Era*. He began by recounting the story of a wealthy
benefactor who told a builder, saying, "Build me a home.
Don't skimp on anything. Forget the cost." The builder did
not live up to the trust. He cut corners, plastered over shoddy
work, and sought to enrich himself by unethical means. When
the home was finished, the builder presented the bills, which
were paid without question, and then was overwhelmed and
chagrined when the wealthy client gave back the keys, saying,

"The home you have just built, my boy, is my present to you."
Elder Wirthlin then went on to tell us how to build our lives
right—how to build upon the real rock:

"The key to building a good life is to center that life on
Christ and his teachings, to '[hear] these sayings of mine, and
[do] them.' If we live the principles of the gospel, we are the
fulfillment of the Savior's pronouncement: 'Ye are the light
of the world' (Matt. 5:14). We can shine among our fellowmen, influencing them to glorify our Father in Heaven. . . . If
we build our lives on service to others and to the Lord, we
are promised the help of the master builder. . . . As you are
building your life, your belief in Christ and his gospel will
guide you the same way that it guides those of us who are still
finishing our building."

After referring to the Ten Commandments and the Golden
Rule, Elder Wirthlin continued, "What a magnificent blueprint for life at its best! These commandments and all that
they encompass constitute a glorious challenge and an unas-
sailable fortress against evil. They involve the use of time in
the best and highest sense and will certainly safeguard our
integrity and morality and help us be a good example. This
is the kind of life building that is possible for Latter-day
Saints. . . .

"If we build our life with and for our Savior, we will build
it from the best materials and with the best effort we can give.
We won't skimp on study or training or diligence or obedience.
We won't misrepresent what we're trying to build. . . . We
will wish to build something noble and solid, something worthy
of the trust we have been given." ("Build It Right," *New Era*,
March 1990, pp. 65–66.)

When we focus on Christ, we truly are building our life
upon an eternal rock. President Thomas S. Monson once said
in a talk in Buenos Aires, a talk for which I was his translator,
that spirituality comes from focusing on Christ every day. He

listed three things we should do in order to draw nearer to the Savior and to grow in spirituality:

1. Fill our minds with thoughts of Christ and the kind of thoughts he wants us to have.

2. Fill our hearts with love of Christ, gratitude for his atoning sacrifice, and love for all mankind as he wants us to do.

3. Fill our lives with service to Christ and to everyone about us; serve as he wants us to serve.

Christ, who learned the trade of carpentry while he was preparing for his ministry, often referred to home building during his mission as he taught the higher laws of living. He spoke of foundations and of the body being "the temple of God." He declared that every house "divided against itself shall not stand" (Matthew 12:25); and, in the Sermon on the Mount, he likened a person's conduct to home building.

The Savior commanded us to "build upon [his] rock, which is [his] gospel." (D&C 11:24), and when he visited the people of Israel in the Americas after his resurrection, he was consistent in using the same imagery of building, declaring: "This is my doctrine, and whoso buildeth upon this buildeth upon my rock, and the gates of hell shall not prevail against them. And whoso shall declare more or less than this, and establish it for my doctrine, the same cometh of evil, and is not built upon my rock; but he buildeth upon a sandy foundation, and the gates of hell stand open to receive such when the floods come and the winds beat upon them." (3 Nephi 11:39–40.)

Helaman, the grandson of Alma, spoke these eternal words to his sons, Nephi and Lehi: "My sons, remember . . . that it is upon the rock of our Redeemer, who is Christ, the Son of God, that ye must build your foundation; that when the devil shall send forth his mighty winds, yea, his shafts in the whirlwind, yea, when all his hail and his mighty storm shall beat upon you, it shall have no power over you to drag you down to the gulf of misery and endless wo, because of the rock upon which ye are built, which is a sure foundation, a foundation whereon if men build they cannot fall." (Helaman 5:12.)

If we build something that we want to last forever, it is imperative to have a firm foundation. To make it secure, we must excavate down to bedrock. This takes time and effort, perseverance, and exactness, but it is requisite to permanency. Thus it is with building our lives upon the rock of Christ. We must follow him, for he has taught us how to build. We cannot take the easy path, hoping to short-circuit laws, and expect to achieve anything permanent and eternal. Building our Christlike life requires active faith, diligence, heed, and endurance.

The Lord declared: "And now, behold, whosoever is of my church, and endureth of my church to the end, him will I establish upon my rock, and the gates of hell shall not prevail against them." (D&C 10:69.) "And, if you keep my commandments and endure to the end you shall have eternal life, which gift is the greatest of all the gifts of God." (D&C 14:7.)

In a revelation given to Joseph Smith in 1832, the Savior said: "Organize yourselves; prepare every needful thing; and establish a house, even a house of prayer, a house of fasting, a house of faith, a house of learning, a house of glory, a house of order, a house of God." (D&C 88:119.) We each can use this pattern in building our own personal "home" — our thoughts, our words, our actions can be "built" after the pattern of this revelation of God. And to make our home with our family more celestial, we also can follow the Master Architect's blueprint that he has provided in this revelation.

President Thomas S. Monson has referred to this revelation from the Lord: "Where could any of us locate a more suitable blueprint whereby he could wisely and properly build? Such a house would meet the building code outlined in Matthew, even a house built 'upon a rock,' . . . a house capable of withstanding the rains of adversity, the floods of opposition, and the winds of doubt everywhere present in our challenging world. . . . Let the Lord be the General Contractor for the family — even the home — we build. Then each of us can be subcontractors responsible for a vital segment of the whole project. All of us are thereby builders." (*Live the Good Life*, p. 124.)

The great prophet of the Restoration, Joseph Smith, summarized his positive attitude about the future of The Church of Jesus Christ of Latter-day Saints, which is built upon the rock of Christ, in these ringing words: "Our missionaries are going forth to different nations. . . . The Standard of Truth has been erected; no unhallowed hand can stop the work from progressing; persecutions may rage, mobs may combine, armies may assemble, calumny may defame, but the truth of God will go forth boldly, nobly, and independent, till it has penetrated every continent, visited every clime, swept every country, and sounded in every ear, till the purposes of God shall be accomplished, and the Great Jehovah shall say the work is done." (*History of the Church* 4:540.)

The personal testimony of every Latter-day Saints is also the rock upon which we stand. The introduction to the Book of Mormon, following the title page, refers to the divine witness, or testimony, that each member has and mentions three parts of that testimony:

1. Jesus Christ is the Savior of the world.

2. Joseph Smith is God's revelator and prophet in these last days (the Book of Mormon proves his divine mission).

3. The Church of Jesus Christ of Latter-day Saints is the Lord's kingdom once again established on the earth preparatory to the second coming of the Messiah. It is the only organization on the face of the earth with the legal power of attorney to

hold the two priesthoods, and with them to perform the saving ordinances established by the Savior as conditions for entering his kingdom and receiving his peace.

The guidelines for daily living given to us by Jesus in the Sermon on the Mount are matchless in helping us to become perfect. These words came from our Savior—from him who has made it possible for every human being to come back into the presence of God and partake of life eternal.

President Howard W. Hunter, in his April 1990 conference address, provides a fitting summary to this book of the Savior's sermon on the mount:

"If we can pattern our life after the Master, and take his teaching and example as the supreme pattern for our own, we will not find it difficult to be consistent and loyal in every walk of life, for we will be committed to a single, sacred standard of conduct and belief. Whether at home or in the marketplace, whether at school or long after school is behind us, whether we are acting totally alone or in concert with a host of other people, our course will be clear and our standards will be obvious. We will have determined, as the prophet Alma said, 'to stand as witnesses of God at all times and in all things, and in all places that [we] may be in, even until death.' (Mosiah 18:9.) . . . [Ultimately,] righteous Christian life requires something more than a contribution. . . . It requires commitment—whole-souled, deeply held, eternally cherished commitment to the . . . commandments God has given." (*Ensign*, May 1990, p. 62.)

Bibliography

Ashton, Marvin J. *Ye Are My Friends.* Salt Lake City: Deseret Book, 1982.

Bennet and Hand. *Designs for Personality.* New York: McGraw-Hill, 1938.

Benson, Ezra Taft. *The Teachings of Ezra Taft Benson.* Salt Lake City: Bookcraft, 1988.

Berrett, William E. *Blessed Are They Who Come unto Me.* Provo, Utah: Ensign Publishing Co., 1979.

Boller, Paul F., Jr. *Presidential Anecdotes.* New York: Oxford University Press, 1981.

Crowell, Grace Noll. *Light of the Years.* New York: Harper and Row, 1964.

Dahl, Larry E. "The Doctrine of Christ." In *The Book of Mormon: Second Nephi, the Doctrinal Structure.* Edited by Monte S. Nyman and Charles D. Tate, Jr. Provo, Utah: Brigham Young University Religious Studies Center, 1989.

Eyring, Henry B. Commencement address at Ricks College, April 21, 1988.

Firmage, Edwin B., ed. *An Abundant Life: The Memoirs of Hugh B. Brown.* Salt Lake City: Signature Books, 1988.

Kimball, Spencer W. *Faith Precedes the Miracle.* Salt Lake City: Deseret Book, 1972.

Lee, Harold B. *Stand Ye in Holy Places.* Salt Lake City: Deseret Book, 1974.

McConkie, Bruce R. *Mormon Doctrine.* 2d ed. Salt Lake City: Bookcraft, 1966.

———. *The Mortal Messiah.* Book 2, *From Bethlehem to Calvary.* Salt Lake City: Deseret Book, 1980.

———. *Doctrinal New Testament Commentary.* Vol. 1, *The Gospels.* Salt Lake City: Bookcraft, 1965.

Monson, Thomas S. *Live the Good Life.* Salt Lake City: Deseret Book, 1988.

Nibley, Hugh. *The Collected Works of Hugh Nibley.* Vol. 4, *Mormonism and Early Christianity.* Edited by Todd M. Compton and Stephen D. Ricks. Salt Lake City: Deseret Book, 1987.

Bibliography

———. *The Collected Works of Hugh Nibley.* Vol. 3, *The World and the Prophets.* Edited by John W. Welch, Gary P. Gillum, and Don E. Norton. Salt Lake City: Deseret Book, 1987.

Oaks, Dallin. *Pure in Heart.* Salt Lake City: Bookcraft, 1988.

Roberts, B. H. *The Seventy's Course in Theology.* 1908.

Saint-Exupéry, Antoine de. *The Little Prince.* New York: Harcourt Brace Jovanovich, 1943.

Smith, Joseph. *Lectures on Faith.* Compiled by N. B. Lundwall. Salt Lake City: Deseret Book, 1985.

———. *Teachings of the Prophet Joseph Smith.* Salt Lake City: Deseret Book, 1976.

Talmage, James E. *Articles of Faith.* Deseret Book, 1984.

———. *Jesus the Christ.* Salt Lake City: Deseret Book, 1983.

Watson, Lillian Eichler, ed. *Light from Many Lamps.* New York: Simon & Schuster, 1951.

Yorgason, Blaine and Brenton. *Receiving Answers to Prayers.* Salt Lake City: Keepsake Bookcards, 1989.

Index

Actions, character involves more than, 79

Adultery: woman taken in, 56; committing, in heart, 71, 116–19

Agency, 187

Aguilar, Esperanza Alvarez de, 178–79

Airplane: flight of, over mountains, 13–14; unresponsive, flown by test pilot, 38–39; piloting, following guidelines in, 185–86

Alma the younger, sin and repentance of, 86–87

Alms: doing, before men, 136–38; accompanying fasting, 145

America: Sermon on Mount repeated in, vii; setting in, for Savior's visit, ix-x

Anderson, Paul, 148

Andes mountains, flight over, 13–14

Anger, avoiding, 84, 114–16

Angels, missionaries likened to, 106

Articles of Faith, 18, 45

Ashton, Marvin J., 138, 159

Ask, and it shall be given, 170–71. *See also* Prayer

Atonement of Jesus Christ: illustrated by story of banker's dilemma, 58; availing ourselves of, 59; scriptures explaining, 59–

61; pondering details of, 62; hymn expressing appreciation for, 62; we are made perfect through, 77; makes peace possible, 87; makes perfection possible, 132

Authority: to bestow Holy Ghost, 48; works done without, 199–200; of priesthood, 200–203; story illustrating need for, 201; possessed by Church, 212–13

Baal, priests of, and Elijah, 171–72

Baby, deformed, doctors warn family about, 178–79

Banker: dilemma of, with justice and mercy, 58; demonstrates need for authority, 201

Baptism, 68; as essential ordinance, 71–72; for dead, 72–73; is gate to strait and narrow path, 188

Beatitudes as requirements for salvation, xi-xii

Benjamin, King, 5–6

Benson, Ezra Taft: on pride, 8–9; on prayer, 142–43; on freedom of choice, 187

Berrett, William E., 97

Blessings, law of, xii

Boasting, sin of, 138

Bok, Edward, 150

217

Book of Mormon: account in, of
Sermon on Mount, vii; purpose
of, to bring people to Christ, xii,
14; verses from, explaining
Atonement, 59–61; using, in
missionary work, 108–9;
introduction to, expresses
testimony, 212–13
Boyle, John, 102
Brazilian song about sorrow, 20
Bronte, Charlotte, 129
Brown, Hugh B., 6, 201
Building upon the rock, 207–13

Calling and election made sure, 78
Carrel, Alexis, 143
Charity: mercy equated with, 64;
sermons on, by Paul and
Mormon, 124–25
Chastening of the Lord, 20–21
Child, becoming as, 6, 32, 190
Chiodo, Beverly, 125–26
Choice, freedom of, 187
Christ's Ideals for Living, 186
Christensen, June, 103
Church of Jesus Christ of Latter-day
Saints: mission of, to bring
people to Christ, xii-xiii, 14;
"less active" members of, 55;
persecution will not destroy, 95;
is hated by world, 96; Book of
Mormon testifies of, 212–13
Clarke, J. Richard, 138–39
Cleansing, ceremonial, 67–68
"Come Thou Fount of Every
Blessing," 160–61
Comfort for those who mourn,
17–18, 19, 25–27
Comforter, second, 78–79
Coming unto Christ, xii, 14; is
source of consolation and
comfort, 25; process of, 71; on
straight and narrow path, 185–90

Commitment, 213
Confucius, 183
Contention, spirit of, 84
Covetousness, 153–54
Cowdery, Oliver, 202–3
Creation, considering, brings
humility, 12
Currant bush, parable of, 6

Dahl, Larry, 188–89
Daniel, 23–24, 99
David's mourning for his sin, 22
Dead: honoring, cultural differences
in, 16–17; typical Latter-day
Saint funeral for, 17–19;
knowing state of, brings comfort,
19; baptism for, 72–73
Debt, avoiding, 155
Decisions, fasting and praying about,
145–47
Desert, story of man crossing, 42–43
Doers of the word, being, 204
Donations, anonymous, 137–38
Down's syndrome children, three
families with, 54

Earth, meek to inherit, 31–33
Earthquake in Mexico City, 111
Elijah and priests of Baal, 171–72
Elisha, 39–40
Ellingson, Diane, story of, 9–12
Enemy, loving, 126–28
Eye for an eye. *See* Retribution, law
of
Eyring, Henry B., 12–13

Faith: trial of, 36; is essential to
peace, 95; sacrifice generates,
155; prayer as manifestation of,
171; and works, 204
False prophets, 191–94
Fasting: hypocrisy in, 144, 146;
accompanied by prayer and

almsgiving, 145; for help in
making decisions, 145–47;
providing for poor through, 147;
blessings of, 148
Featherstone, Vaughn J., 125–26
Fechter, Christl, 127–28
Food, brethren deliver, through
gunfire, 111–12
Forgiveness: receiving blessing of,
22–23; extending, relieves our
own burdens, 56; of others brings
peace, 88; through loving
enemies, 127–28; we must
extend in order to receive, 143–
44, 165; and not judging, 165.
See also Mercy
Foundation, firm, building upon,
207–13
Freedom of choice, 187
Funerals, 17–19

Gandhi, meekness of, 37
Gifts of the Spirit, 46–47, 176
God: indebtedness to, 4–5; ways of,
are not our ways, 16, 28; worship
of, in funeral services, 18;
submitting to will of, 32, 34–35;
trust in, 35; following direction
of, 35–36; mercy of, man's need
for, 63; privilege of seeing, 66–
67, 74–79; was seen by ancient
and modern prophets, 77; peace
depends on, 85; becoming
children of, 88–89; man cannot
serve mammon and, 156–59;
love of, is greatest
commandment, 181–82
Golden questions, 106–7
Golden Rule, 180–84
Good Samaritan: parable of, 63;
following example of, 110–12
Greeks, ancient, 195–96
Gymnast's recovery from accident,
story of, 9–12

Haight, David B., 180–81
Happiness versus blessedness, 14
"Have I Done Any Good," 139
Heart, mighty change in, 69
Hedberg, Kathleen, 102
Hinckley, Gordon B., 121–22
Hipwell, M.B., 122
Holy Ghost: being filled with, 43–
44, 46; fruits of, 46–47; functions
of, 47–48; authority to bestow,
48; withdraws from angry
persons, 114–15; gift of, 176
Home: establishing peace in, 82–83;
combatting worldly influences in,
119; unethical builder of, story
of, 208–9
Horse trainer in Argentina, 29
House, building, upon rock, 207–13
Humility, 4–6; counseled by Alma,
7; illustrated in parable of
Pharisee and publican, 7; defined
as being teachable, 7–8, 12–13,
34; methods for attaining, 8–9;
following trials, 9; engendered by
weaknesses, 12, 33–34; in
considering vastness of creation,
12; and meekness, 32–34
Hungering and thirsting after
righteousness, 42–43; blessings
following, 43–44, 46; developing
habit of, 44–45; losing habit of,
46; and temple blessings, 48–50;
and missionary service, 50–51;
assessing level of, 51
Hunter, Howard W., 213
Hypocrisy, 69–70, 73; acts
performed in, are not rewarded
by God, 135, 205–6; Savior
denounces, 135–36; in
almsgiving, 136–38; in praying,
140–42; in fasting, 144, 146

"I Stand All Amazed," 62

Importunate host, parable of, 172–73

"In Fasting We Approach Thee," 148

Isaiah, 145, 148

Jesus Christ: baptism and ministry of, viii; coming unto, xii-xiii, 14; condemned having "respect to persons," 4; faith in, comforts those who mourn, 18, 26–27; yoke of, is easy, 25; unconditional love of, for us, 53; mercy demonstrated by, 56, 65; postresurrection teachings of, 72–73; as second Comforter, 78–79; becoming sons and daughters of, 88–89; persecution of, 94–95; becoming perfect in, 131; following, through service, 139; we do not pray to, 142; pathway to, is narrow, 185–90; is only way to salvation, 189–90; testimony of, is spirit of prophecy, 193; focusing on, 209–10. *See also* Atonement of Jesus Christ

Jesus the Christ, 18

Job, perspective of, on suffering, 21

John the Beloved, 50–51, 105

Joseph of Egypt, 75, 99

Judgment: avoiding, 162–64, 167; difficulty of, due to individual reality, 165–66; leaving, to God, 167

Justice, demands of, met by Savior, 58–59

Justin Martyr, 196–97

Kimball, Spencer W., 33–34, 118–19, 145

Kingdom of God, seeking first, 160–61, 176

Language, clean, 121–23

Latin Americans, generosity of, 110–12, 161

Law of Moses, Jesus compares, with new law, 113–14

Lazarus and rich man, parable of, 2–4

Lee, Harold B.: on indebtedness to God, 4–5; on forgiveness, 22–23; on meekness, 36; on mercy, 52; on seeing God through being pure, 74–75; interview with, about Vietnam War, 81–82; on persecution, 97; on receiving answers to prayer, 178

Lepers, Christ's mercy to, 56

Light: of world, being, 101–2; having whole body filled with, 103

Lincoln, Abraham, 57–58

Little Prince, The, 30

"Lord, I Would Follow Thee," 169

Lord's Prayer, 141

Love: sacrifice begets, 53–54, 159; involves living higher law, 124; sermons on, by Paul and Mormon, 124–25; for enemies, 126–28; of all people, 130–31; demonstrating, through service, 139; as greatest commandment, 181–82; Golden Rule is based on, 183

Lust, 116–19

Mahatma Gandhi, meekness of, 37

Mammon, man cannot serve God and, 156–59

Marriage is ordained of God, 117

Martyrs, 90, 96–97

Mary (mother of Jesus), meekness of, 37–38

Masters, two, man cannot serve, 156–59

Materialism. *See* Riches

McConkie, Bruce R.: on poor in spirit, 5; on inheritance of earth by meek, 31; on mercy, 54–55; on seeing God, 66–67; on peacemakers, 83; on persecution, 95–97; on becoming perfect, 133–34; on praying to Christ, 142; on *strait* and *straight*, 187; on priesthood authority, 200

McKay, David O., 135–36

Meekness: seeming undesirability of, in world, 28; defined as *manso* or tame, 29–31; of Savior, 31; and inheritance of earth, 31–32; implies submitting to will of God, 32, 34–37; and humility, 32–34; strength in, 36; scriptural and historical examples of, 37–38; and retaliation, 41; as self-mastery, 41

Merchant of Venice, 56–57

Mercy: our salvation rests upon, 52; we must show, to obtain it ourselves, 52–53, 54–55; begotten by sacrifice and service, 53; consequences of lack of, 55–56; demonstrated by Savior, 56; described in quotation from Shakespeare, 56–57; shown by Abraham Lincoln, 57–58; illustrated in story of banker's dilemma, 58; Christ paid for, with Atonement, 58–59; of God, man's need for, 63; of humans for one another, 63–64; equated with charity, 64; Old Testament references to, 64; sure promises of, 64–65

Merrell, V. Dallas, President and Sister, 102–3

Mexico City, earthquake in, 111

Missionaries likened to angels, 106

Missionary work: desires for, 50–51, 105; likened to salt of earth, 100–101; involves being light to world, 101–2; by every member, suggestions on, 102–4, 106–7; setting goals in, 103; scriptural commandments regarding, 104; John's desire for, 105; key to, is working with members, 105–6; golden questions in, 106–7; examples of member's success in, 107–8; through sharing Book of Mormon, 108–9; through bringing people to sacrament meeting, 109–10; abandoning riches for, 155–56

Monson, Thomas S., 209–10, 211–12

Mormon, mourning of, for people's sins, 25

Mortality, tribulation as part of, 21

Moses, meekness of, 37

Mountains: flight over, 13–14; holy, as place of communion with God, 50

Mourning: purpose in, 15–16, 21; over death of loved one, 16–21; permanence of, 20; as universal experience, 20–21; for our own sins, 21–23; for sins of others, 23–25

Murder, and anger, 114–16

Naaman the Syrian, 39–40

Nephi, son of Helaman, 24–25

Nibley, Hugh, 72–73, 193–94, 195–98

Oaks, Dallin H., 49, 79, 112, 152, 205

Oath-taking, 119–21

Obedience: examples illustrating, 38–40; prosperity through, 152

Ordinances: authority to perform, 202; without works, 204

Packer, Boyd K., 50, 153
Parents, love and sacrifice of, 53
Paul: meekness of, 38; persecutions endured by, 91–92
Peace: promised by Christ, 65, 81–82, 85–86; establishing, in home, 82–83; learning to live in, during mortality, 83–84; unity and harmony in, 84–85; First Presidency statement on, 85; absence of, in sinning, 86; of repentance, 86–87; made possible by Atonement, 87; and reconciliation, 87–88; through forgiving others, 88
Peacemakers: as doers, not just hearers, of word, 80; Lord's disciples are, 83; opposite of, 83; missionaries as, 87–88; to become children of God, 88–89
Perfection: blueprint for, given by Jesus, vii; through submission to God's will, xiii; commandment to achieve, 130–34; depends on Atonement, 132; in one's own sphere, 132–33; long process of, 133–34
Persecution: blessings of, in next life, 90, 97, 99; endured by Paul, 91–92; of Stephen, 92; of Joseph Smith, 92–94; of Jesus, 94–95; inevitability of, 95, 97; will not destroy Church, 95; various types of, 97–98; greatest defense against, 98–99
Phair, Kendra Kasl, 9–12
Pharisee and publican, parable of, 7, 203
Pioneers, dedication of, 161
Plan of salvation: peace and comfort in, 18, 19; having trust in, 35; scriptures explaining, 59–61
Plato, 194
Polo ponies, example of, 38
Poor: Savior's compassion for, 4; in spirit, definition of, 4–5; faith of, 5; caring for, 137; providing for, through fast offerings, 145, 147
Pornography, 118–19
Poverty: likely, of Christ's family, 1; and spirituality, 152–53
Prayer: to be seen of men, 7; of widowed mother, 19–20; hypocritical, 140; the Lord's, 141; public, guidelines for, 141–42; directed inappropriately to Christ, 142; suggestions concerning, 142–43; and fasting, 145–46, 175; as manifestation of faith, 171; continuing in, 172–73; is commanded of God, 173–74; in faith, belief, and sincerity, 174; appropriate requests in, 174–75; recognizing answers to, 177–78
Prejudice, 168
Pride, 8–9
Priesthood authority, 200–203
Profanity, 121–23
Prophets: mourning of, for people's sins, 24–25; living, belief in, 191–92, 196–97; preferring past, to present, 197. *See also* False prophets
Publican: and Pharisee, parable of, 7, 203; description of, 130
Purity of heart: definition of, 66, 67–69, 79; blessings accompanying, 66–67, 74–76; and self-review, 69–70; and sexual purity, 70–71; scriptures concerning, 73–74; leads to seeing God, 74–79

Reconciliation, 87–88, 115

Relationships, "taming" each other in, 31

Religious tolerance, 167–68

Repentance: sorrow that worketh, 22–23; peace available through, 86–87

"Respect to persons," Savior's condemnation of, 4

Retribution, law of, 40–41; replaced by new law, 85, 123–26, 129

Rich man and Lazarus, parable of, 2–4

Rich young ruler, 2

Riches: tendency for wealthy to focus on, 1–2; proper use of, 2, 152; encumbrance of, 5, 155; treasuring, above things of God, 150–51; addictive nature of, 151; turning away from, 151–52, 158; love of, 153–54; working excessively to obtain, 154

Righteousness: hungering and thirsting after, 42–43; as fruit of the Spirit, 47; seeking, rather than manifestations, 177

Roberts, B.H., 46–47

Rock, building upon, 207–13

Romney, Marion G., 75

Sacrament meeting, bringing nonmembers to, 109–10

Sacrifice: love begotten by, 53–54; generates faith, 155

Saint-Exupéry, Antoine de, 30

Salt of earth: missionary work as, 100–101; becoming, through service, 110–12

Samaritan, Good: parable of, 63; following example of, 110–12

Scriptures: examples of meekness from, 37–38; explaining Atonement, 59–61

Second mile, going, 125–26

Seeking the Lord, 175–77

Self-control, 129

Sermon on the Mount: as blueprint for perfection, vii; repeated on American continent, vii; setting for, vii–ix; American setting for, ix–x; various translations of, x–xi; teaches putting aside things of world, xiii

Service, 110–12; performing, to be seen of men, 136–38; shows our love for Savior, 139; begets love, 159

Sexual purity, 70–71, 116–19

Shakespeare, William, 56–57

Shalom, 80–81

"Should You Feel Inclined to Censure," 166

Sins: mourning for, 20–25; "unimportant," stressed in Savior's new law, 113–14; retaining remission of, 137

Smith, Joseph: appetite of, for knowledge, 46; temples planned and built by, 49; persecution of, 92–94; on sacrifice, 155; on receiving answers to prayer, 178; on false versus true prophets, 192–93; priesthood authority of, 202–3; on rolling forth of work, 212; Book of Mormon testifies of, 212

Smith, Winifred, 122

Socrates, 194

Solon of Athens, 195

Sorrow: understanding purpose in, 15–16, 21; Brazilian song about, 20; godly, worketh repentance, 22–23. *See also* Mourning

Spirituality: and riches, 21, 152–53; level of, seeing God depends on, 75–76; comes from focusing on Christ, 209–10

Straight and narrow path, 185–90

Talmage, James E.: on setting for Sermon on Mount, vii–viii; on Lazarus and rich man, 2–3; on mourning, 15; writings of, 18, 45; on unforgiving servant, 55–56; on oath-taking, 120–21; on becoming perfect, 132–33; on serving two masters, 156–57; on acting in name of Lord, 200; on priesthood authority, 202–3; on building upon rock, 208

Tame, *meek* as synonym for, 30–31

Tanner, Obert C., 186

Temple: desire for blessings of, 48–50; symbolic ordinances of, 68; body as, 74

Test pilot, example of, 38–39

Testimony, three elements of, 212–13

Tolerance, 165–67; of religious beliefs, 167–68

Treasures, laying up, in heaven, 149–50. *See also* Riches

Trees blown down in storm, 73

Trial of faith, 36

Tribulation as necessary part of mortality, 21

Trust, 35

"Truth Reflects upon Our Senses," 163–64

Two masters, man cannot serve, 156–59

Unforgiving servant, parable of, 53, 55–56, 144, 164–65

Unity, 84

Unworthiness, acknowledging, before God, 7

Vietnam War, reporters interview President Lee about, 81–82

Von Harnack, Adolf, 73

Weaknesses, God gives, to promote humility, 12, 33–34

Wealth. *See* Riches

Wells, Edwin, 120

Wells, Elayne, 128

Wells, Helen, 164–67

"Who come unto me," addition of phrase, xii, 14

Widow, prayers of, for comfort, 19–20

Winder, Barbara, 147

Wirthlin, Joseph B., 208–9

Wisdom, seeking for, 176

Work, prudent, importance of, 154–55, 157

Works: hypocritical, vanity of, 135–36, 205–6; doing, to be seen of men, 136–38; done in Lord's name without authority, 199–200; importance of, 204

World: putting aside things of, xiii; Saints hated by, 96; seeking praise of, 154–55

Yorgason, Blaine and Brenton, 117–18, 177

Zoroaster, 183